Decoding the TOEFL® iBT

Actual Test

READING 2

INTRODUCTION

For many learners of English, the TOEFL® iBT will be the most important standardized test they ever take. Unfortunately for a large number of these individuals, the material covered on the TOEFL® iBT remains a mystery to them, so they are unable to do well on the test. We hope that by using the *Decoding the TOEFL® iBT* series, individuals who take the TOEFL® iBT will be able to excel on the test and, in the process of using the book, may unravel the mysteries of the test and therefore make the material covered on the TOEFL® iBT more familiar to themselves.

The TOEFL® iBT covers the four main skills that a person must learn when studying any foreign language: reading, listening, speaking, and writing. The *Decoding the TOEFL® iBT* series contains books that cover all four of these skills. The *Decoding the TOEFL® iBT* series contains books with three separate levels for all four of the topics, and it also contains *Decoding the TOEFL® iBT Actual Test* books. These books contain several actual tests that learners can utilize to help them become better prepared to take the TOEFL® iBT. This book, *Decoding the TOEFL® iBT Actual Test Reading 2*, covers the reading aspect of the test and includes reading passages that are arranged in the same format as the TOEFL® iBT. Finally, the TOEFL® iBT underwent a number of changes in August 2019. This book—and the others in the series—takes those changes into account and incorporates them in the texts and questions, so readers of this second edition can be assured that they have up-to-date knowledge of the test.

Decoding the TOEFL® iBT Actual Test Reading 2 can be used by learners who are taking classes and also by individuals who are studying by themselves. It contains a total of nine full-length reading actual tests. Each actual test contains three reading passages. All of the passages are the same length and have the same difficulty levels as those found on the TOEFL® iBT. In addition, the passages contain the same numbers and types of questions that appear on the actual TOEFL® iBT, and the questions also have the same difficulty levels as those found on the TOEFL® iBT. Individuals who use *Decoding the TOEFL® iBT Actual Test Reading 2* will therefore be able to prepare themselves not only to take the TOEFL® iBT but also to perform well on the test.

We hope that everyone who uses *Decoding the TOEFL® iBT Actual Test Reading 2* will be able to become more familiar with the TOEFL® iBT and will additionally improve his or her score on the test. As the title of the book implies, we hope that learners can use it to crack the code on the TOEFL® iBT, to make the test itself less mysterious and confusing, and to get the highest score possible. Finally, we hope that both learners and instructors can use this book to its full potential. We wish all of you the best of luck as you study English and prepare for the TOEFL® iBT, and we hope that *Decoding the TOEFL® iBT Actual Test Reading 2* can provide you with assistance during the course of your studies.

Michael A. Putlack
Stephen Poirier
Allen C. Jacobs

TABLE
OF
CONTENTS

ABOUT THE TOEFL® iBT READING SECTION

Changes in the Reading Section

TOEFL® underwent many changes in August of 2019. The following is an explanation of the changes that have been made to the Reading section.

Format

The number of passages that appear in the Reading section is either 3 or 4. The time given for the Reading section is either 54 (3 passages) or 72 (4 passages) minutes.

Passages

The length of each passage has been slightly shortened. A typical Reading passage is between 690 and 710 words. However, there are some passages with as few as 670 words.

In addition, there is a heavier emphasis on science topics. This includes topics such as biology, zoology, and astronomy.

There are sometimes pictures accompanying the text. They are used to provide visual evidence of various objects discussed in the passage. On occasion, there are also pictures used for glossary words.

The glossary typically defines 0-2 words or phrases.

Questions

There are only 10 questions per Reading passage now. This is a decrease from the 12-14 questions that were asked on previous tests.

Question Types

TYPE 1 Vocabulary Questions

Vocabulary questions require the test taker to understand specific words and phrases that are used in the passage. Each of these questions asks the test taker to select another word or phrase that is the most similar in meaning to a word or phrase that is highlighted. The vocabulary words that are highlighted are often important words, so knowing what these words mean can be critical for understanding the entire passage. The highlighted words typically have several different meanings, so test takers need to be careful to avoid selecting an answer choice simply because it is the most common meaning of the word or phrase.

- There are 1-3 Vocabulary questions per passage.
- Passages typically have 2 Vocabulary questions.

TYPE 2 Reference Questions

Reference questions require the test taker to understand the relationships between words and their referents in the passage. These questions most frequently ask the test taker to identify the antecedent of a pronoun. In many instances, the pronouns are words such as *he, she,* or *they* or *its, his, hers,* or *theirs.* However, in other instances, relative pronouns such as which or demonstrative pronouns such as *this* or *that* may be asked about instead.

- There are 0-1 Reference questions per passage. However, these questions rarely appear anymore.

TYPE 3 Factual Information Questions

Factual Information questions require the test taker to understand and be able to recognize facts that are mentioned in the passage. These questions may be about any facts or information that is explicitly covered in the passage. They may appear in the form of details, definitions, explanations, or other kinds of data. The facts which the questions ask about are typically found only in one part of the passage—often just in a sentence or two in one paragraph—and do not require a comprehensive understanding of the passage as a whole.

- There are 1-3 Factual Information questions per passage. There is an average of 2 of these questions per passage.
- Some Factual Information questions require test takers to understand the entire paragraph, not just one part of it, to find the correct answer.

TYPE 4 Negative Factual Information Questions

Negative Factual Information questions require the test taker to understand and be able to recognize facts that are mentioned in the passage. These questions may be about any facts or information that is explicitly covered in the passage. However, these questions ask the test taker to identify the incorrect information in the answer choices. Three of the four answer choices therefore contain correct information that is found in the passage. The answer the test taker must choose therefore either has incorrect information or information that is not mentioned in the passage.

- There are 0-2 Negative Factual Information questions per passage.

TYPE 5 Sentence Simplification Questions

Sentence Simplification questions require the test taker to select a sentence that best restates one that has been highlighted in the passage. These questions ask the test taker to recognize the main points in the sentence and to make sure that they are mentioned in the rewritten sentence. These rewritten sentences use words, phrases, and grammar that are different from the highlighted sentence. Sentence Simplification questions do not always appear in a passage. When they are asked, there is only one Sentence Simplification question per passage.

- There are 0-1 Sentence Simplification questions per passage.
- The answer choices for these questions are approximately half the length of the sentences being asked about.

TYPE 6 Inference Questions

Inference questions require the test taker to understand the argument that the passage is attempting to make. These questions ask the test taker to consider the information that is presented and then to come to a logical conclusion about it. The answers to these questions are never explicitly stated in the passage. Instead, the test taker must infer what the author means. These questions often deal with cause and effect or comparisons between two different things, ideas, events, or people.

- There are 0-2 Inference questions per passage. Most passages have at least 1 Inference question though.
- The difficulty level of these questions has increased. In some cases, test takers must be able to understand an entire paragraph rather than only a part of it.

TYPE 7 Rhetorical Purpose Questions

Rhetorical Purpose questions require the test taker to understand why the author mentioned or wrote about something in the passage. These questions ask the test taker to consider the reasoning behind the information being presented in the passage. For these questions, the function—not the meaning—of the material is the most important aspect for the test taker to be aware of. The questions often focus on the relationship between the information mentioned or covered either in paragraphs or individual sentences in the passage and the purpose or intention of the information that is given.

- There are 1-2 Rhetorical Purpose questions per passage.
- There is a special emphasis on these questions. Some questions ask about entire sentences, not just words or phrases.

TYPE 8 Insert Text Questions

Insert Text questions require the test taker to determine where in the passage another sentence should be placed. These questions ask the test taker to consider various aspects, including grammar, logic, connecting words, and flow, when deciding where the new sentence best belongs. Insert Text questions do not always appear in a passage. When they are asked, there is only one Insert Text question per passage. This question always appears right before the last question.

- There are 0-1 Insert Text questions per passage.
- There is a special emphasis on these questions. Almost every passage now has 1 Insert Text question.

TYPE 9 Prose Summary Questions

Prose Summary questions require the test taker to understand the main point of the passage and then to select sentences which emphasize the main point. These questions present a sentence which is essentially a thesis statement for the entire passage. The sentence synthesizes the main points of the passage. The test taker must then choose three out of six sentences that most closely describe points mentioned in the introductory sentence. As for the other three choices, they describe minor points, have incorrect information, or contain information that does not appear in the passage, so they are all therefore incorrect. This is always the last question asked about a Reading passage, but it does not always appear. Instead, a Fill in a Table question may appear in its place.

- There are 0-1 Prose Summary questions per passage.
- There is a special emphasis on these questions. Almost every passage now has 1 Prose Summary question.

TYPE 10 Fill in a Table Questions

Fill in a Table questions require the test taker to have a comprehensive understanding of the entire passage. These questions typically break the passage down into two—or sometimes three—main points or themes. The test taker must then read a number of sentences or phrases and determine which of the points or themes the sentences or phrases refer to. These questions may ask the test taker to consider cause and effect, to compare and contrast, or to understand various theories or ideas covered. This is always the last question asked about a Reading passage, but it does not always appear. Instead, a Prose Summary question may appear in its place.

- There are 0-1 Fill in a Table questions per passage.
- These questions rarely appear anymore. Prose Summary questions are much more common than Fill in a Table questions.

Actual Test

01

Reading Section Directions

This section measures your ability to understand academic passages in English. You will have **54 minutes** to read and answer questions about **3 passages**. A clock at the top of the screen will show you how much time is remaining.

Most questions are worth 1 point but the last question for each passage is worth more than 1 point. The directions for the last question indicate how many points you may receive.

Some passages include a word or phrase that is <u>underlined</u>. Click on the word or phrase to see a definition or an explanation.

When you want to move to the next question, click on **NEXT**. You may skip questions and go back to them later. If you want to return to previous questions, click on **BACK**. You can click on **REVIEW** at any time, and the review screen will show you which questions you have answered and which you have not answered. From this review screen, you may go directly to any question you have already seen in the Reading section.

Click on **CONTINUE** to go on.

Earth's Carbon Cycle

Virtually all life on the Earth depends upon two gases: oxygen and carbon dioxide. Humans and animals inhale oxygen and exhale carbon dioxide whereas plant life respires carbon dioxide and releases oxygen. Organisms utilize these gases to make their nutrition systems function properly; therefore, maintaining the current levels of the two gases in the atmosphere is essential to nearly all life on the planet. This is particularly true of carbon dioxide because, if its level rises too much, radical changes in the environment, which could endanger all life on the Earth, may occur. At present, the atmosphere consists roughly of 78% nitrogen, 21% oxygen, and trace amounts of several other gases, including carbon dioxide, which comprises around 0.03% of the atmosphere. The current level of carbon dioxide is maintained by the carbon cycle, through which carbon dioxide that is put into the atmosphere is subsequently removed in various ways.

The majority of the carbon dioxide found on the planet was created in the Earth's interior when it formed billions of years ago and remains trapped there. Resultantly, the main source of carbon dioxide is outgassing from inside the planet. It reaches the atmosphere by escaping through surface volcanoes and cracks in the underwater mid-ocean ridges. It can also get into the atmosphere from changes in <u>carbonate rocks</u> in the crust that have absorbed carbon dioxide. The carbon dioxide that enters the atmosphere is disseminated in a number of manners. For example, a large amount is held as biomass in dead and decaying plant matter that is slowly transforming into sedimentary rocks such as limestone or which forms coal seams and petroleum pools. More is dissolved in the oceans, where it is bound in carbonate rocks, and a small amount simply remains in the atmosphere.

The plant biomass storage of carbon dioxide begins with photosynthesis. Plants extract carbon dioxide from the atmosphere and use it to create energy for themselves, but a small amount remains inside them. Whenever plants die, decay, and get covered with layers of sediment, that carbon dioxide is buried. In addition, every time plants perform photosynthesis, oxygen in its gaseous form is created as a byproduct. This oxygen is released into the atmosphere and inhaled by humans and animals. When they exhale, they breathe out carbon dioxide. Over the hundreds of millions of years that life has existed on the planet, the exchange of carbon dioxide and oxygen has favored the latter and has resulted in the atmosphere containing a high level of oxygen and an extremely minor amount of carbon dioxide.

Another major reason there is so much more oxygen than carbon dioxide concerns a process called weathering. A large amount of carbon dioxide gets dissolved in ocean waters, where it combines with water to form carbonic acid. The acid, in turn, separates into hydrogen <u>ions</u> and bicarbonate ions, which react with minerals in ocean rocks. This alters, or weathers, the ocean rocks and creates carbonate rocks. Due to these reactions, a portion of atmospheric carbon dioxide gets stored in rocks—typically layers of

limestone—in the ocean. Then, another process returns some carbon dioxide to the atmosphere. Erosion of the ocean floors and of former ocean floors that are presently exposed as surface land releases the stored-up carbon dioxide in the carbonate rocks and returns it to the atmosphere, whereupon the cycle repeats itself.

The carbon cycle has kept the level of carbon dioxide relatively low for millions of years. Unfortunately, mankind has affected the carbon cycle primarily by extracting enormous amounts of stored carbon dioxide from the Earth in the form of coal and petroleum. The burning of these fossil fuels for energy has increased the levels of carbon dioxide and other gases such as sulfur in the atmosphere. In addition, there are many places around the world that are being deforested. This is particularly true in areas such as the Amazon Rainforest in South America and rainforests in Southeast Asia. As a result, the overall amount of plant biomass has been reduced, so there are fewer plants to absorb carbon dioxide and to transform it into oxygen. This has resulted in the gradual altering of the planet's carbon cycle, which may ultimately have dire consequences for the future of life on the Earth.

*Glossary

carbonate rock: a rock that has carbonate ions in it

ion: an electrically charged particle

1   According to paragraph 1, which of the following is NOT true about the Earth's atmosphere?

(A) The carbon cycle enables it to maintain a constant amount of carbon dioxide.

(B) It contains greater amounts of carbon dioxide than it does hydrogen.

(C) There are two elements which comprise the vast majority of it.

(D) The maintaining of the gases in it helps keep organisms on the Earth alive.

Paragraph 1 is marked with an arrow (➡).

2   The word "disseminated" in the passage is closest in meaning to

(A) abandoned

(B) reduced

(C) distributed

(D) identified

Earth's Carbon Cycle

➡ Virtually all life on the Earth depends upon two gases: oxygen and carbon dioxide. Humans and animals inhale oxygen and exhale carbon dioxide whereas plant life respires carbon dioxide and releases oxygen. Organisms utilize these gases to make their nutrition systems function properly; therefore, maintaining the current levels of the two gases in the atmosphere is essential to nearly all life on the planet. This is particularly true of carbon dioxide because, if its level rises too much, radical changes in the environment, which could endanger all life on the Earth, may occur. At present, the atmosphere consists roughly of 78% nitrogen, 21% oxygen, and trace amounts of several other gases, including carbon dioxide, which comprises around 0.03% of the atmosphere. The current level of carbon dioxide is maintained by the carbon cycle, through which carbon dioxide that is put into the atmosphere is subsequently removed in various ways.

The majority of the carbon dioxide found on the planet was created in the Earth's interior when it formed billions of years ago and remains trapped there. Resultantly, the main source of carbon dioxide is outgassing from inside the planet. It reaches the atmosphere by escaping through surface volcanoes and cracks in the underwater mid-ocean ridges. It can also get into the atmosphere from changes in carbonate rocks in the crust that have absorbed carbon dioxide. The carbon dioxide that enters the atmosphere is disseminated in a number of manners. For example, a large amount is held as biomass in dead and decaying plant matter that is slowly transforming into sedimentary rocks such as limestone or which forms coal seams and petroleum pools. More is dissolved in the oceans, where it is bound in carbonate rocks, and a small amount simply remains in the atmosphere.

*Glossary

carbonate rock: a rock that has carbonate ions in it

3 The author discusses "photosynthesis" in order to

- Ⓐ explain the roles of carbon dioxide and oxygen in the process
- Ⓑ point out how much carbon dioxide plants need to undergo it
- Ⓒ stress the value of the oxygen that plants release into the atmosphere
- Ⓓ discuss the manner in which it enables carbon dioxide to enter the ground

4 Which of the sentences below best expresses the essential information in the highlighted sentence in the passage? Incorrect answer choices change the meaning in important ways or leave out essential information.

Over the hundreds of millions of years that life has existed on the planet, the exchange of carbon dioxide and oxygen has favored the latter and has resulted in the atmosphere containing a high level of oxygen and an extremely minor amount of carbon dioxide.

- Ⓐ Carbon dioxide has been released into the atmosphere in great quantities; however, an even larger amount of oxygen has been produced and let into the air as well.
- Ⓑ In a process taking millions of years to occur, oxygen was produced in vast amounts through the process of photosynthesis, so there is a higher level of it than there is carbon dioxide.
- Ⓒ Since life first appeared on the Earth, more oxygen than carbon dioxide has been released into the atmosphere, so there is a much greater amount of oxygen in the air at present.
- Ⓓ Because there is a small amount of carbon dioxide in the atmosphere, a much greater amount of oxygen has been able to be released over a period of hundreds of millions of years.

The plant biomass storage of carbon dioxide begins with photosynthesis. Plants extract carbon dioxide from the atmosphere and use it to create energy for themselves, but a small amount remains inside them. Whenever plants die, decay, and get covered with layers of sediment, that carbon dioxide is buried. In addition, every time plants perform photosynthesis, oxygen in its gaseous form is created as a byproduct. This oxygen is released into the atmosphere and inhaled by humans and animals. When they exhale, they breathe out carbon dioxide. Over the hundreds of millions of years that life has existed on the planet, the exchange of carbon dioxide and oxygen has favored the latter and has resulted in the atmosphere containing a high level of oxygen and an extremely minor amount of carbon dioxide.

5 According to paragraph 3, which of the following is true about photosynthesis?

Ⓐ Not all of the carbon dioxide that plants respire is used during the process.

Ⓑ It is the only reason there is so much oxygen in the Earth's atmosphere.

Ⓒ Plants are able to use it to extract carbon dioxide from the ground.

Ⓓ It cannot be undergone by plants unless there is a sufficient amount of sunlight.

Paragraph 3 is marked with an arrow (➡).

6 According to paragraph 4, weathering occurs when

Ⓐ carbonate rocks release the carbon dioxide stored in them

Ⓑ carbon dioxide from the atmosphere gets dissolved by ocean water

Ⓒ certain kinds of rocks are instilled with carbon dioxide

Ⓓ carbonic acid is divided into two different types of ions

Paragraph 4 is marked with an arrow (⇨).

➡ The plant biomass storage of carbon dioxide begins with photosynthesis. Plants extract carbon dioxide from the atmosphere and use it to create energy for themselves, but a small amount of it remains inside them. Whenever plants die, decay, and get covered with layers of sediment, that carbon dioxide is buried. In addition, every time plants perform photosynthesis, oxygen in its gaseous form is created as a byproduct. This oxygen is released into the atmosphere and inhaled by humans and animals. When they exhale, they breathe out carbon dioxide. Over the hundreds of millions of years that life has existed on the planet, the exchange of carbon dioxide and oxygen has favored the latter and has resulted in the atmosphere containing a high level of oxygen and an extremely minor amount of carbon dioxide.

⇨ Another major reason there is so much more oxygen than carbon dioxide concerns a process called weathering. A large amount of carbon dioxide gets dissolved in ocean waters, where it combines with water to form carbonic acid. The acid, in turn, separates into hydrogen <u>ions</u> and bicarbonate ions, which react with minerals in ocean rocks. This alters, or weathers, the ocean rocks and creates carbonate rocks. Due to these reactions, a portion of atmospheric carbon dioxide gets stored in rocks—typically layers of limestone—in the ocean. Then, another process returns some carbon dioxide to the atmosphere. Erosion of the ocean floors and of former ocean floors that are presently exposed as surface land releases the stored-up carbon dioxide in the carbonate rocks and returns it to the atmosphere, whereupon the cycle repeats itself.

*Glossary

ion: an electrically charged particle

7   The word "dire" in the passage is closest in
     meaning to

   Ⓐ potential

   Ⓑ various

   Ⓒ terrible

   Ⓓ far-reaching

8   Which of the following can be inferred from
     paragraph 5 about carbon dioxide?

   Ⓐ It exists in the atmosphere in lower
        amounts when the Earth has more
        forested areas.

   Ⓑ It is presently being created more through
        mankind's actions than it is by natural
        means.

   Ⓒ Increasing amounts of it in the
        atmosphere have caused some species
        to become extinct.

   Ⓓ The rising levels of it are responsible
        for the recent increase in the planet's
        temperature.

   Paragraph 5 is marked with an arrow (➡).

➡ The carbon cycle has kept the level of
carbon dioxide relatively low for millions of years.
Unfortunately, mankind has affected the carbon
cycle primarily by extracting enormous amounts
of stored carbon dioxide from the Earth in the
form of coal and petroleum. The burning of these
fossil fuels for energy has increased the levels of
carbon dioxide and other gases such as sulfur in
the atmosphere. In addition, there are many places
around the world that are being deforested. This
is particularly true in areas such as the Amazon
Rainforest in South America and rainforests in
Southeast Asia. As a result, the overall amount of
plant biomass has been reduced, so there are fewer
plants to absorb carbon dioxide and to transform it
into oxygen. This has resulted in the gradual altering
of the planet's carbon cycle, which may ultimately
have dire consequences for the future of life on the
Earth.

More Available

9   Look at the four squares [■] that indicate where the following sentence could be added to the passage.

In fact, some extensive eruptions are capable of spewing vast amounts of carbon dioxide into the air.

Where would the sentence best fit?

Click on a square [■] to add the sentence to the passage.

The majority of the carbon dioxide found on the planet was created in the Earth's interior when it formed billions of years ago and remains trapped there. **1** Resultantly, the main source of carbon dioxide is outgassing from inside the planet. **2** It reaches the atmosphere by escaping through surface volcanoes and cracks in the underwater mid-ocean ridges. **3** It can also get into the atmosphere from changes in carbonate rocks in the crust that have absorbed carbon dioxide. **4** The carbon dioxide that enters the atmosphere is disseminated in a number of manners. For example, a large amount is held as biomass in dead and decaying plant matter that is slowly transforming into sedimentary rocks such as limestone or which forms coal seams and petroleum pools. More is dissolved in the oceans, where it is bound in carbonate rocks, and a small amount simply remains in the atmosphere.

*Glossary

carbonate rock: a rock that has carbonate ions in it

10 Directions: An introductory sentence for a brief summary of the passage is provided below. Complete the summary by selecting the THREE answer choices that express the most important ideas of the passage. Some sentences do not belong because they express ideas that are not presented in the passage or are minor ideas in the passage. **This question is worth 2 points.**

> Drag your answer choices to the spaces where they belong. To remove an answer choice, click on it. To review the passage, click on **VIEW TEXT**.

Carbon dioxide enters and departs the Earth's atmosphere in a number of ways in what is known as the carbon cycle.

-
-
-

ANSWER CHOICES

1. The actions of humans, such as burning fossil fuels, are removing large amounts of carbon dioxide from the air.

2. When plants perform photosynthesis, they create oxygen as a byproduct and release it into the air.

3. In the oceans, weathering can cause carbon dioxide to enter various types of rocks to create carbonate rocks.

4. The amount of carbon dioxide has been kept much lower than that of oxygen for millions of years.

5. Great amounts of carbon dioxide escape from the Earth's interior and reach the atmosphere.

6. There are only trace amounts of carbon dioxide in the atmosphere while there are large amounts of nitrogen and oxygen.

The Evidence for a Liquid Ocean on Europa

water plumes on Europa detected by the *Galileo* space probe

Europa is one of the numerous moons orbiting Jupiter and is the sixth closest one to the gas giant. It is nearly the same size as Earth's moon, yet while it has a rugged, pitted landscape of craters and mountains, Europa has one of the smoothest surfaces of any celestial body ever observed. This is on account of Europa having a surface comprised primarily of frozen water. While there are some surface cracks and fissures, it almost completely lacks craters. The great amount of water on its surface has led astronomers to speculate it may contain an interior liquid ocean. Most of the evidence, of which there are three main types, comes from long-range observations as well as a few flybys by space probes.

Europa is believed to have a solid iron core with a rocky mantle and a layer of water around the mantle. Tidal heating, which is caused by the strong gravitational pull of Jupiter, may result in this layer of water being mostly liquid beneath the moon's frozen exterior. Europa orbits Jupiter swiftly as it takes only three and a half Earth days to complete a single rotation around the gargantuan planet. Europa's orbit is not quite a perfect circle, so the slight eccentricity in its orbit causes Jupiter's gravity to pull on it at varying levels of strength. One result is that when Europa is at perigee to Jupiter, it is pulled in a slightly more elongated shape toward the planet. However, when Europa is at apogee from Jupiter, its shape reverts to one that is more spherical. The pulling and retracting result in the creating of a tidal force of gravity, which causes a great amount of heating in Europa's core and mantle. It is on account of this heat that many astronomers believe the interior ocean of the moon is in a constant liquid state rather than a frozen one.

Another piece of evidence that astronomers frequently cite is the existence of water plumes on Europa. These are geysers of water expelled from the interior of Europa to a distance approximately 200 kilometers above the moon's surface. If all of the water on Europa were frozen, then these plumes would not form. Instead, astronomers hypothesize that water heated by tidal forces is pushed up from below,

whereupon it bursts through the ice and goes into space. These plumes only erupt when Europa is at apogee from Jupiter and after it has undergone a period of intense tidal stress.

The third piece of evidence mentioned by numerous astronomers is the nature of the fissures located on Europa's surface. These fissures suggest that there is a tremendous amount of activity underneath the surface. Some astronomers liken the activity to the plate tectonics affecting the Earth's surface. Large sections of Europa's icy surface appear to be moving, so they crash into, push against, and move away from one another similar to how the plates on the Earth's crust behave. It is most likely that the driving mechanism of the movements of the ice plates is warm water beneath the icy crust. As the waters of Europa are heated by tidal gravitational forces, they rise and fall, which creates convection forces that push warm water to the surface. This not only forms water plumes but also forms cracks in the surface, where warm water spills out and then freezes to form the large fissures on Europa's surface.

Astronomers who believe there is a liquid interior ocean on Europa posit that it is enormous. Some even theorize that it could contain more than twice the amount of water found in all the Earth's oceans combined. Whether it is a freshwater ocean or has high concentrations of minerals that would make it salty like the Earth's oceans is unknown though. What is also unknown is whether extraterrestrial life exists there; however, many astronomers consider Europa to be a prime candidate for alien life. This speculation may be resolved in the near future as the European Space Agency is scheduled to launch a probe to Europa in 2022, and NASA, the American space agency, is preparing a similar mission. High on the agenda for both missions are searches for a liquid interior ocean and for extraterrestrial life.

*Glossary

perigee: the point at which a celestial object is at its closest to the object it orbits
apogee: the point at which a celestial object is at its farthest from the object it orbits

Beginning ▲

11 The author discusses "Earth's moon" in order
to

    Ⓐ explain why it has so many craters while
Europa mostly lacks them

    Ⓑ point out why it is so comparable in size
to Europa

    Ⓒ compare the appearance of its surface
with that of Europa's

    Ⓓ discuss the possibility that it may have an
interior ocean like Europa

12 According to paragraph 1, which of the
following is true about Europa?

    Ⓐ It has more water in frozen form on its
surface than in liquid form beneath it.

    Ⓑ There is currently a space probe that is in
constant orbit around it.

    Ⓒ It is one of Jupiter's largest moons and
was among the first to be discovered.

    Ⓓ Astronomers have been able to observe it
up close on a number of occasions.

Paragraph 1 is marked with an arrow (➡).

The Evidence for a Liquid Ocean on Europa

➡ Europa is one of the numerous moons orbiting
Jupiter and is the sixth closest one to the gas giant.
It is nearly the same size as Earth's moon, yet
while it has a rugged, pitted landscape of craters
and mountains, Europa has one of the smoothest
surfaces of any celestial body ever observed.
This is on account of Europa having a surface
comprised primarily of frozen water. While there
are some surface cracks and fissures, it almost
completely lacks craters. The great amount of water
on its surface has led astronomers to speculate it
may contain an interior liquid ocean. Most of the
evidence, of which there are three main types,
comes from long-range observations as well as a
few flybys by space probes.

More Available ▲

13 According to paragraph 2, Europa changes shape because

(A) the path of its orbit causes Jupiter's gravity to affect it with varying strength

(B) the great amount of water in its oceans causes severe tidal heating

(C) the heat in the moon's core and mantle makes its surface alter constantly

(D) its swift orbit and closeness to Jupiter make it vulnerable to the planet's gravity

Paragraph 2 is marked with an arrow (➡).

14 The word "intense" in the passage is closest in meaning to

(A) powerful

(B) regulated

(C) constant

(D) extended

15 According to paragraph 3, the water plumes on Europa most likely occur because

(A) Jupiter's powerful gravitational pull attracts liquid water beneath the surface

(B) the strength of the tides on Europa causes great masses of water to go into space

(C) underwater volcanoes heat the water and then spew it above the surface

(D) warm liquid water in the interior is forced to the surface and then ejected

Paragraph 3 is marked with an arrow (⇨).

➡ Europa is believed to have a solid iron core with a rocky mantle and a layer of water around the mantle. Tidal heating, which is caused by the strong gravitational pull of Jupiter, may result in this layer of water being mostly liquid beneath the moon's frozen exterior. Europa orbits Jupiter swiftly as it takes only three and a half Earth days to complete a single rotation around the gargantuan planet. Europa's orbit is not quite a perfect circle, so the slight eccentricity in its orbit causes Jupiter's gravity to pull on it at varying levels of strength. One result is that when Europa is at perigee to Jupiter, it is pulled in a slightly more elongated shape toward the planet. However, when Europa is at apogee from Jupiter, its shape reverts to one that is more spherical. The pulling and retracting result in the creating of a tidal force of gravity, which causes a great amount of heating in Europa's core and mantle. It is on account of this heat that many astronomers believe the interior ocean of the moon is in a constant liquid state rather than a frozen one.

⇨ Another piece of evidence that astronomers frequently cite is the existence of water plumes on Europa. These are geysers of water expelled from the interior of Europa to a distance approximately 200 kilometers above the moon's surface. If all of the water on Europa were frozen, then these plumes would not form. Instead, astronomers hypothesize that water heated by tidal forces is pushed up from below, whereupon it bursts through the ice and goes into space. These plumes only erupt when Europa is at apogee from Jupiter and after it has undergone a period of intense tidal stress.

*Glossary

perigee: the point at which a celestial object is at its closest to the object it orbits

apogee: the point at which a celestial object is at its farthest from the object it orbits

REVIEW

HELP

BACK

NEXT

HIDE TIME 00:54:00

End

16 Why does the author mention "plate tectonics"?

Ⓐ To help explain how the fissures on Europa's surface are formed

Ⓑ To note that both Earth and Europa are affected by its actions

Ⓒ To discuss why the convection forces on Europa are so enormous

Ⓓ To compare the crust of Europa with that of the Earth

17 According to paragraph 4, what is believed to be the cause of the movement of the ice on the surface of Europa?

Ⓐ The gravitational pull of Jupiter on the moon

Ⓑ The action of tectonic plates in the crust of Europa

Ⓒ Earthquakes that are centered in the mantle of Europa

Ⓓ Heated liquid water lying beneath the moon's surface

Paragraph 4 is marked with an arrow (➡).

18 The word "prime" in the passage is closest in meaning to

Ⓐ preferable

Ⓑ leading

Ⓒ apparent

Ⓓ plausible

➡ The third piece of evidence mentioned by numerous astronomers is the nature of the fissures located on Europa's surface. These fissures suggest that there is a tremendous amount of activity underneath the surface. Some astronomers liken the activity to the plate tectonics affecting the Earth's surface. Large sections of Europa's icy surface appear to be moving, so they crash into, push against, and move away from one another similar to how the plates on the Earth's crust behave. It is most likely that the driving mechanism of the movements of the ice plates is warm water beneath the icy crust. As the waters of Europa are heated by tidal gravitational forces, they rise and fall, which creates convection forces that push warm water to the surface. This not only forms water plumes but also forms cracks in the surface, where warm water spills out and then freezes to form the large fissures on Europa's surface.

Astronomers who believe there is a liquid interior ocean on Europa posit that it is enormous. Some even theorize that it could contain more than twice the amount of water found in all the Earth's oceans combined. Whether it is a freshwater ocean or has high concentrations of minerals that would make it salty like the Earth's oceans is unknown though. What is also unknown is whether extraterrestrial life exists there; however, many astronomers consider Europa to be a prime candidate for alien life. This speculation may be resolved in the near future as the European Space Agency is scheduled to launch a probe to Europa in 2022, and NASA, the American space agency, is preparing a similar mission. High on the agenda for both missions are searches for a liquid interior ocean and for extraterrestrial life.

19 Look at the four squares [■] that indicate where the following sentence could be added to the passage.

Since life on the Earth is believed to have originated in the oceans, some believe that a liquid ocean on Europa could also harbor some type of life.

Where would the sentence best fit?

Click on a square [■] to add the sentence to the passage.

➡ Astronomers who believe there is a liquid interior ocean on Europa posit that it is enormous. Some even theorize that it could contain more than twice the amount of water found in all the Earth's oceans combined. **1** Whether it is a freshwater ocean or has high concentrations of minerals that would make it salty like the Earth's oceans is unknown though. **2** What is also unknown is whether extraterrestrial life exists there; however, many astronomers consider Europa to be a prime candidate for alien life. **3** This speculation may be resolved in the near future as the European Space Agency is scheduled to launch a probe to Europa in 2022, and NASA, the American space agency, is preparing a similar mission. **4** High on the agenda for both missions are searches for a liquid interior ocean and for extraterrestrial life.

20 **Directions:** An introductory sentence for a brief summary of the passage is provided below. Complete the summary by selecting the THREE answer choices that express the most important ideas of the passage. Some sentences do not belong because they express ideas that are not presented in the passage or are minor ideas in the passage. **This question is worth 2 points.**

Drag your answer choices to the spaces where they belong. To remove an answer choice, click on it. To review the passage, click on **VIEW TEXT**.

Astronomers believe there is a high likelihood that an interior liquid ocean exists on Jupiter's moon Europa for a number of reasons.

-
-
-

ANSWER CHOICES

1. Water beneath Europa's surface is likely heated and forced to the surface, where it is then ejected into outer space.

2. The unique orbit that Europa has around Jupiter causes the planet's gravity to affect it in a variety of ways.

3. Jupiter's gravity causes tidal heating in Europa's interior, so it is speculated that this heat makes it warm enough for water to be liquid.

4. The large fissures which appear on the surface of Europa are probably caused by large sheets of ice being moved by water beneath them.

5. Many astronomers believe there is a great chance that some form of life exists somewhere in Europa's interior ocean.

6. The surface of Europa is incredibly smooth, which is a great contrast with the surface of Earth's moon, which has many craters.

The South Sea Bubble of 1720

The South Sea Bubble of 1720 is the moniker given to an economic crisis that happened due to speculation on stocks centering on the South Sea Company of England. In less than a year, shares of the company increased in value roughly ten times, which caused a frenzy of activity as investors sought to become wealthy by buying or selling the company's stock. This resulted in a ripple effect as more companies attempted to benefit in a similar manner. Ultimately, however, the South Sea Company's stock collapsed in 1720, which not only reduced many of its investors to states of penury but also caused widespread economic troubles in England and elsewhere.

In 1711, Robert Harley, the Chancellor of the Exchequer of England, and businessman John Blunt founded the South Sea Company to fund the English government's debt. At that time, England was incurring huge debts on account of its involvement in the War of Spanish Succession, which lasted from 1701 to 1713. Harley and Blunt concluded that the best way to control the country's financial obligations was to raise money through a joint-stock bank in which wealthy individuals could invest and then to use the funds obtained to cover the government's debt. However, due to the fact that the Bank of England's charter permitted it to be the only <u>joint-stock bank</u> in England, the two had to find another method. They decided to create a firm that would resemble a trading company on the surface but would, in actuality, be a secret mechanism to pay off England's debt.

The new South Sea Company was granted a monopoly on all trade in the South Seas region, which at that time referred to the Spanish colonies in the Americas. With the government's sanction for the scheme, Harley and Blunt convinced many affluent investors to purchase ten million pounds' worth of shares. For their initial investments, these individuals would receive an annuity of 6%. The government intended to pay it with tariffs from trading ships that brought goods from the South Seas region. Unfortunately, when the War of Spanish Succession concluded in 1713, the terms of the peace treaty allowed the English to send only one trading ship to the Spanish colonies each year. This was granted to the South Sea Company but was a tremendous disappointment since Harley and Blunt had expected the company to obtain more extensive trading rights.

Despite this, the company proceeded with its operations and even raised an additional two million pounds in 1717. The plan seemed to be working fine as investors somehow received a 6% return each year. Nevertheless, the English government's debt continued rising, and, by 1719, it owed its creditors approximately fifty million pounds. Three of them—the Bank of England, the East India Company, and the South Sea Company—were due a combined 18.3 million pounds. Then, the South Sea Company's directors proposed to take on half of the government's debt with an issue of new shares. They attracted new investors by spreading rumors of a fabulous amount of wealth in gold and silver waiting to be taken from the Spanish colonies.

Their <u>rumormongering</u> sparked a frenzy of speculative investment. The value of a share in the company rose in value from 128 pounds in January 1720 to nearly 1,000 pounds by August. Blunt even allowed investors to borrow money from the South Sea Company to purchase shares in the company. At the same time, numerous others took advantage of the situation and established their own joint-stock companies, most of which had dubious plans for their investors' funds. These companies were nicknamed "bubbles" as they seemed destined to be short-lived ventures. Nonetheless, they managed to attract investors, and the mania rapidly spread to the European mainland.

When it suddenly became common knowledge that the South Sea Company was not as profitable as had been claimed, the value of the company's stock plummeted from 1,000 to 150 pounds in less than a month. Many people—especially those who had borrowed money to purchase shares—went bankrupt. Since large numbers of these shareholders could no longer pay off their debts, widespread bankruptcy became the order of the day not just in England but also in Europe and the Americas.

*Glossary

joint-stock bank: a bank that issues stock and whose investors are responsible for any debts it incurs

rumormongering: the malicious spreading of stories or gossip that is not true

21 The word "penury" in the passage is closest in meaning to

(A) displacement

(B) anger

(C) poverty

(D) confusion

22 The author discusses "the War of Spanish Succession" in order to

(A) describe the effects it had on the economies of various European countries

(B) point out how the English got involved in that war for more than a decade

(C) show the way that it harmed some sectors of the English economy and banking system

(D) explain the manner in which it affected the finances of the English government

23 According to paragraph 2, which of the following is true about Robert Harley and John Blunt?

(A) Both men became wealthy by going into business with each other.

(B) They worked to find a way to rid the English government of its financial obligations.

(C) Their involvement in the War of Spanish Succession caused considerable harm to England.

(D) They were two of the more famous founders of the Bank of England.

Paragraph 2 is marked with an arrow (➡).

The South Sea Bubble of 1720

The South Sea Bubble of 1720 is the moniker given to an economic crisis that happened due to speculation on stocks centering on the South Sea Company of England. In less than a year, shares of the company increased in value roughly ten times, which caused a frenzy of activity as investors sought to become wealthy by buying or selling the company's stock. This resulted in a ripple effect as more companies attempted to benefit in a similar manner. Ultimately, however, the South Sea Company's stock collapsed in 1720, which not only reduced many of its investors to states of penury but also caused widespread economic troubles in England and elsewhere.

➡ In 1711, Robert Harley, the Chancellor of the Exchequer of England, and businessman John Blunt founded the South Sea Company to fund the English government's debt. At that time, England was incurring huge debts on account of its involvement in the War of Spanish Succession, which lasted from 1701 to 1713. Harley and Blunt concluded that the best way to control the country's financial obligations was to raise money through a joint-stock bank in which wealthy individuals could invest and then to use the funds obtained to cover the government's debt. However, due to the fact that the Bank of England's charter permitted it to be the only joint-stock bank in England, the two had to find another method. They decided to create a firm that would resemble a trading company on the surface but would, in actuality, be a secret mechanism to pay off England's debt.

*Glossary

joint-stock bank: a bank that issues stock and whose investors are responsible for any debts it incurs

24 The phrase "sanction for" in the passage is closest in meaning to

(A) regulation of

(B) awareness of

(C) involvement in

(D) approval of

25 According to paragraph 3, which of the following is NOT true about the South Sea Company?

(A) It sent expeditions to the Spanish colonies at various times throughout the year.

(B) It was granted a monopoly on trade with a region that belonged to Spain.

(C) It received an initial investment that amounted to ten million pounds.

(D) It intended to pay all of its investors a specific amount on a yearly basis.

Paragraph 3 is marked with an arrow (➡).

26 In paragraph 4, the author suggests that the directors of the South Sea Company

(A) had large amounts of money personally invested in the company

(B) attempted to gain more investors by spreading false information

(C) managed to attract many of the East India Company's biggest investors

(D) intended to pay their investors back with both gold and silver

Paragraph 4 is marked with an arrow (⇨).

➡ The new South Sea Company was granted a monopoly on all trade in the South Seas region, which at that time referred to the Spanish colonies in the Americas. With the government's sanction for the scheme, Harley and Blunt convinced many affluent investors to purchase ten million pounds' worth of shares. For their initial investments, these individuals would receive an annuity of 6%. The government intended to pay it with tariffs from trading ships that brought goods from the South Seas region. Unfortunately, when the War of Spanish Succession concluded in 1713, the terms of the peace treaty allowed the English to send only one trading ship to the Spanish colonies each year. This was granted to the South Sea Company but was a tremendous disappointment since Harley and Blunt had expected the company to obtain more extensive trading rights.

⇨ Despite this, the company proceeded with its operations and even raised an additional two million pounds in 1717. The plan seemed to be working fine as investors somehow received a 6% return each year. Nevertheless, the English government's debt continued rising, and, by 1719, it owed its creditors approximately fifty million pounds. Three of them—the Bank of England, the East India Company, and the South Sea Company—were due a combined 18.3 million pounds. Then, the South Sea Company's directors proposed to take on half of the government's debt with an issue of new shares. They attracted new investors by spreading rumors of a fabulous amount of wealth in gold and silver waiting to be taken from the Spanish colonies.

27 In stating that the value of the company's stock "plummeted," the author means that the stock

(A) could not be traded

(B) became worthless

(C) was seized by the authorities

(D) decreased rapidly in price

28 According to paragraph 6, there were financial problems in Europe and America because

(A) the South Sea Company lost a great deal of money and then went out of business

(B) both English and Spanish colonies in the Americas were not as productive as possible

(C) a large number of companies in those places went bankrupt in 1720

(D) numerous shareholders in the South Sea Company were unable to pay their debts

Paragraph 6 is marked with an arrow (➡).

Their rumormongering sparked a frenzy of speculative investment. The value of a share in the company rose in value from 128 pounds in January 1720 to nearly 1,000 pounds by August. Blunt even allowed investors to borrow money from the South Sea Company to purchase shares in the company. At the same time, numerous others took advantage of the situation and established their own joint-stock companies, most of which had dubious plans for their investors' funds. These companies were nicknamed "bubbles" as they seemed destined to be short-lived ventures. Nonetheless, they managed to attract investors, and the mania rapidly spread to the European mainland.

➡ When it suddenly became common knowledge that the South Sea Company was not as profitable as had been claimed, the value of the company's stock plummeted from 1,000 to 150 pounds in less than a month. Many people—especially those who had borrowed money to purchase shares— went bankrupt. Since large numbers of these shareholders could no longer pay off their debts, widespread bankruptcy became the order of the day not just in England but also in Europe and the Americas.

*Glossary

rumormongering: the malicious spreading of stories or gossip that is not true

29 Look at the four squares [■] that indicate where the following sentence could be added to the passage.

Even individuals across the Atlantic Ocean in the American colonies found themselves eager to invest in these companies.

Where would the sentence best fit?

Click on a square [■] to add the sentence to the passage.

Their <u>rumormongering</u> sparked a frenzy of speculative investment. The value of a share in the company rose in value from 128 pounds in January 1720 to nearly 1,000 pounds by August. Blunt even allowed investors to borrow money from the South Sea Company to purchase shares in the company. ■ At the same time, numerous others took advantage of the situation and established their own joint-stock companies, most of which had dubious plans for their investors' funds. ■ These companies were nicknamed "bubbles" as they seemed destined to be short-lived ventures. ■ Nonetheless, they managed to attract investors, and the mania rapidly spread to the European mainland. ■

*Glossary

rumormongering: the malicious spreading of stories or gossip that is not true

30 **Directions:** An introductory sentence for a brief summary of the passage is provided below. Complete the summary by selecting the THREE answer choices that express the most important ideas of the passage. Some sentences do not belong because they express ideas that are not presented in the passage or are minor ideas in the passage. **This question is worth 2 points.**

> Drag your answer choices to the spaces where they belong. To remove an answer choice, click on it. To review the passage, click on **VIEW TEXT**.

In 1720, the value of the South Sea Company increased dramatically but then dropped just as quickly, which caused economic problems in a number of places.

-
-
-

ANSWER CHOICES

1. Robert Harley and John Blunt were the two men who were primarily involved in the founding of the South Sea Company.

2. The bankruptcies caused by the South Sea Company resulted in a number of negative issues in Europe and America.

3. The South Sea Company was established in order to help the government of England raise a large amount of money from investors.

4. The people in charge of the South Sea Company spread false reports in order to increase the value of the company.

5. The War of Spanish Succession had a major effect on the founding and running of the South Sea Company.

6. Upon the discovery that the South Sea Company was not highly profitable, the value of its shares declined instantly.

32

Actual Test

02

Reading Section Directions

This section measures your ability to understand academic passages in English. You will have **54 minutes** to read and answer questions about **3 passages**. A clock at the top of the screen will show you how much time is remaining.

Most questions are worth 1 point but the last question for each passage is worth more than 1 point. The directions for the last question indicate how many points you may receive.

Some passages include a word or phrase that is underlined. Click on the word or phrase to see a definition or an explanation.

When you want to move to the next question, click on **NEXT**. You may skip questions and go back to them later. If you want to return to previous questions, click on **BACK**. You can click on **REVIEW** at any time, and the review screen will show you which questions you have answered and which you have not answered. From this review screen, you may go directly to any question you have already seen in the Reading section.

Click on **CONTINUE** to go on.

The Chinese Taiping Rebellion

the retaking of Nanjing by Qing troops

From 1850 to 1864, one of the most horrific rebellions in recorded history took place as warfare raged across large parts of Southern China. To this day, it is uncertain how many people died, but conservative estimates put the number at twenty million. The rebellion was initiated as a religious crusade led by Hong Xiuquan, who established an independent state in Southern China and began enacting reforms that attracted numerous followers. Eventually, the ruling Qing Dynasty was obligated to request assistance from foreign mercenaries to quell the rebellion.

Hong Xiuquan was a member of a minority group called the Hakka, a branch of the dominant Han Chinese ethnic group. As such, his people often found themselves marginalized in Chinese society. Despite this disadvantage, Hong desired to join the ranks of the Chinese government; however, he failed the civil service entrance examination several times. After his last failure in 1847, he became ill. While sick, he claimed to have received a vision declaring he was a younger sibling of Jesus Christ. Hong had already been influenced by Christianity, which was being spread by foreign missionaries in China.

After recovering from his illness, Hong formed a religious sect that quickly gained many adherents. During the late 1840s, the sect became influential in Southern China by protecting civilians from bandits and pirates. The group's ranks were further swelled by individuals disaffected by the ineffective national government. They were particularly incensed by its inability to protect China from the growing impact of various Western powers that wanted to add parts of China to their large overseas empires.

By 1850, the Qing rulers decided that Hong's influence had grown too much, so they determined to suppress his sect. This decision resulted in open armed conflict and years of bloodshed. In 1851, Hong's sect defeated a small Qing army, and Hong consequently established an independent state called the Taiping Heavenly Kingdom. In 1853, the Taiping forces captured the city of Nanjing on the Yangtze River

and made it the kingdom's capital. Hong then began implementing a series of reforms to strengthen his position. He established the notion of common property, which had strong support by the rural peasantry, who typically worked for wealthy landlords and lived at near-starvation levels most of their lives. Hong also banned alcohol, tobacco, and the usage of opium, gave more rights to women, increased literacy, and organized his kingdom to make it an efficient political and military state.

Unfortunately for Hong, he made a crucial mistake after capturing Nanjing. He paused to consolidate his forces, which numbered nearly one million, and to start his reform programs. In doing so, he granted a respite to the Qing Dynasty that enabled it to gather more forces. Furthermore, he upset some of his followers once he began living a life of luxury in Nanjing. Hong's proto-Christian beliefs pushed away many middle-class Chinese, who were bound to traditional Confucian ideas, and his radical reforms won him no converts among the wealthy, who believed they would lose both their land and riches under a China ruled by Hong. Hong additionally failed to win any foreign support, a move that proved to be an integral factor in the rebellion's next stage.

In 1856, the Taiping forces were rocked by internal revolts as Hong was obligated to put down dissent among many of his disillusioned followers. The fact that Hong's supporters were divided should have been the turning point in the rebellion. But in the same year, the long-simmering conflict between the West and China erupted into the Second Opium War, which lasted until 1860. The Qing Dynasty was simply unable to defeat the Taiping rebels while simultaneously battling the French and British. The tide turned, however, in August 1860, when the rebels were defeated while trying to take Shanghai. The Second Opium War ended soon afterward, and the Qing rulers hired foreign mercenaries, including many experienced British and American officers, to lead the Qing armies. By 1864, the revitalized Qing armies had pushed the rebels back to Nanjing. That June, Hong died, either from food poisoning or suicide, and the city fell in July. These two events marked the defeat of the rebels and the end of the bloody rebellion.

*Glossary

marginalize: to put in a position of less power or influence

missionary: a person who travels somewhere and attempts to convert others to his or her religion

1 The word "quell" in the passage is closest in meaning to

Ⓐ battle

Ⓑ placate

Ⓒ handle

Ⓓ suppress

2 According to paragraph 2, which of the following is NOT true about Hong Xiuquan?

Ⓐ He had a religious experience during a time when he was ill.

Ⓑ He was unable to pass a test despite taking it multiple times.

Ⓒ He was a low-ranking member of the Chinese civil service.

Ⓓ He belonged to an ethnic group that had little power in China.

Paragraph 2 is marked with an arrow (➡).

The Chinese Taiping Rebellion

From 1850 to 1864, one of the most horrific rebellions in recorded history took place as warfare raged across large parts of Southern China. To this day, it is uncertain how many people died, but conservative estimates put the number at twenty million. The rebellion was initiated as a religious crusade led by Hong Xiuquan, who established an independent state in Southern China and began enacting reforms that attracted numerous followers. Eventually, the ruling Qing Dynasty was obligated to request assistance from foreign mercenaries to quell the rebellion.

➡ Hong Xiuquan was a member of a minority group called the Hakka, a branch of the dominant Han Chinese ethnic group. As such, his people often found themselves marginalized in Chinese society. Despite this disadvantage, Hong desired to join the ranks of the Chinese government; however, he failed the civil service entrance examination several times. After his last failure in 1847, he became ill. While sick, he claimed to have received a vision declaring he was a younger sibling of Jesus Christ. Hong had already been influenced by Christianity, which was being spread by foreign missionaries in China.

*Glossary

marginalize: to put in a position of less power or influence
missionary: a person who travels somewhere and attempts to convert others to his or her religion

3 The word "adherents" in the passage is closest in meaning to

Ⓐ onlookers

Ⓑ supporters

Ⓒ soldiers

Ⓓ donors

4 In paragraph 3, the author implies that many members of Hong Xiuquan's sect

Ⓐ had traveled abroad and were familiar with foreign customs

Ⓑ were considered outlaws and were pursued by law enforcement officials

Ⓒ disliked the influence that foreign countries had in China

Ⓓ believed that China should attempt to colonize other nations

Paragraph 3 is marked with an arrow (➡).

5 According to paragraph 4, which of the following is true about the Taiping Heavenly Kingdom?

Ⓐ It received some support from various members of the Qing Dynasty.

Ⓑ It was founded in the year 1850 and used the city of Nanjing as its capital.

Ⓒ It came into being as the result of a military conquest in a rebellion.

Ⓓ It significantly improved the lives of the poor individuals living in it.

Paragraph 4 is marked with an arrow (⇨).

➡ After recovering from his illness, Hong formed a religious sect that quickly gained many adherents. During the late 1840s, the sect became influential in Southern China by protecting civilians from bandits and pirates. The group's ranks were further swelled by individuals disaffected by the ineffective national government. They were particularly incensed by its inability to protect China from the growing impact of various Western powers that wanted to add parts of China to their large overseas empires.

⇨ By 1850, the Qing rulers decided that Hong's influence had grown too much, so they determined to suppress his sect. This decision resulted in open armed conflict and years of bloodshed. In 1851, Hong's sect defeated a small Qing army, and Hong consequently established an independent state called the Taiping Heavenly Kingdom. In 1853, the Taiping forces captured the city of Nanjing on the Yangtze River and made it the kingdom's capital. Hong then began implementing a series of reforms to strengthen his position. He established the notion of common property, which had strong support by the rural peasantry, who typically worked for wealthy landlords and lived at near-starvation levels most of their lives. Hong also banned alcohol, tobacco, and the usage of opium, gave more rights to women, increased literacy, and organized his kingdom to make it an efficient political and military state.

Q
REVIEW

?
HELP

‹
BACK

›
NEXT

HIDE TIME 00:54:00

More Available ▲

6 Which of the sentences below best expresses the essential information in the highlighted sentence in the passage? Incorrect answer choices change the meaning in important ways or leave out essential information.

Hong's proto-Christian beliefs pushed away many middle-class Chinese, who were bound to traditional Confucian ideas, and his radical reforms won him no converts among the wealthy, who believed they would lose both their land and riches under a China ruled by Hong.

Ⓐ Hong was a Christian, and he tried to make changes in Chinese society based upon both land ownership and money.

Ⓑ The reforms and beliefs of Hong were disliked by both members of the middle class and the wealthy in China.

Ⓒ Because Hong's reforms caused the wealthy to lose land and money, they did not support Hong at all.

Ⓓ While the middle class sometimes supported Hong and his reforms, the rich were strongly opposed to them.

Unfortunately for Hong, he made a crucial mistake after capturing Nanjing. He paused to consolidate his forces, which numbered nearly one million, and to start his reform programs. In doing so, he granted a respite to the Qing Dynasty that enabled it to gather more forces. Furthermore, he upset some of his followers once he began living a life of luxury in Nanjing. Hong's proto-Christian beliefs pushed away many middle-class Chinese, who were bound to traditional Confucian ideas, and his radical reforms won him no converts among the wealthy, who believed they would lose both their land and riches under a China ruled by Hong. Hong additionally failed to win any foreign support, a move that proved to be an integral factor in the rebellion's next stage.

End

7   Why does the author mention "the Second Opium War"?

Ⓐ To explain how it affected the Qing Dynasty in its fight against Hong Xiuquan

Ⓑ To claim that it posed a greater threat to the Qing Dynasty than Hong Xiuquan did

Ⓒ To explain how so many foreign mercenaries came to be stationed in China

Ⓓ To describe one of the major battles which took place during that war

8   According to paragraph 6, the Qing employed foreign mercenaries because

Ⓐ the soldiers that were hired were experienced at besieging cities

Ⓑ the Qing leaders wanted them to be in charge of their forces

Ⓒ the Qing lacked enough trained troops to fight a modern war

Ⓓ the mercenaries were needed to train the Qing soldiers to fight

Paragraph 6 is marked with an arrow (➡).

➡ In 1856, the Taiping forces were rocked by internal revolts as Hong was obligated to put down dissent among many of his disillusioned followers. The fact that Hong's supporters were divided should have been the turning point in the rebellion. But in the same year, the long-simmering conflict between the West and China erupted into the Second Opium War, which lasted until 1860. The Qing Dynasty was simply unable to defeat the Taiping rebels while simultaneously battling the French and British. The tide turned, however, in August 1860, when the rebels were defeated while trying to take Shanghai. The Second Opium War ended soon afterward, and the Qing rulers hired foreign mercenaries, including many experienced British and American officers, to lead the Qing armies. By 1864, the revitalized Qing armies had pushed the rebels back to Nanjing. That June, Hong died, either from food poisoning or suicide, and the city fell in July. These two events marked the defeat of the rebels and the end of the bloody rebellion.

9 Look at the four squares [■] that indicate where the following sentence could be added to the passage.

This was merely the beginning of his successful occupying of land within China itself.

Where would the sentence best fit?

Click on a square [■] to add the sentence to the passage.

By 1850, the Qing rulers decided that Hong's influence had grown too much, so they determined to suppress his sect. This decision resulted in open armed conflict and years of bloodshed. In 1851, Hong's sect defeated a small Qing army, and Hong consequently established an independent state called the Taiping Heavenly Kingdom. **1** In 1853, the Taiping forces captured the city of Nanjing on the Yangtze River and made it the kingdom's capital. **2** Hong then began implementing a series of reforms to strengthen his position. **3** He established the notion of common property, which had strong support by the rural peasantry, who typically worked for wealthy landlords and lived at near-starvation levels most of their lives. **4** Hong also banned alcohol, tobacco, and the usage of opium, gave more rights to women, increased literacy, and organized his kingdom to make it an efficient political and military state.

10 **Directions:** An introductory sentence for a brief summary of the passage is provided below. Complete the summary by selecting the THREE answer choices that express the most important ideas of the passage. Some sentences do not belong because they express ideas that are not presented in the passage or are minor ideas in the passage. **This question is worth 2 points.**

Drag your answer choices to the spaces where they belong. To remove an answer choice, click on it. To review the passage, click on **VIEW TEXT**.

The Chinese Taiping Rebellion happened due to the actions of Hong Xiuquan but ultimately resulted in the defeat of both him and his forces.

-
-
-

ANSWER CHOICES

1. The army of Hong Xiuquan defeated a Qing army and then established a state called the Taiping Heavenly Kingdom.

2. By using mercenaries from other countries, the Qing defeated the forces of Hong Xiuquan and ended the rebellion.

3. Hong Xiuquan established a religious sect that became very powerful in part of Southern China.

4. The Qing rulers had to fight the forces of Hong Xiuquan and those of European powers at the same time during the 1860s.

5. Hong Xiuquan had a religious experience that made him believe he was related to Jesus Christ.

6. Thanks to all of the reforms made by Hong Xiuquan, many wealthy and influential Chinese began to support his rebellion.

Daniel Defoe and His Writings

One of the founders of both modern English journalism and literature is English writer Daniel Defoe. While primarily known for being a journalist and pamphleteer in his early years, he later attained fame for his novels, particularly *Robinson Crusoe*, *A Journal of the Plague Year*, and *Moll Flanders*. Born to an affluent family of candle merchants in London, England, in 1660, Defoe finished his education and went into business dealing commodities such as wool and wine. Despite some business success, Defoe was plagued with debt issues for practically his entire life, which had a deleterious effect on him, his wife, and his eight children. While he engaged in business for decades, he considered himself a writer and political activist rather than a businessman.

Many of Defoe's early writings dealt with the political and social issues of his time. The most prominent of these was the Glorious Revolution of 1688, which toppled King James II from the English throne. As a result of the revolution, William of Orange, the ruler of the Netherlands and husband of James's daughter Mary, became the king of England. A staunch defender of the revolution, Defoe wrote several pamphlets defending William's right to rule. His most famous one, entitled *A True-Born Englishman*, was printed in 1701 and defended the king against racial attacks by his enemies. They claimed the king had no right to rule because he was Dutch and, accordingly, not a true Englishman. Defoe's pamphlet challenged the English people's belief that they were a pure race by pointing out that they were descended from many foreign tribes. Although his writing won Defoe favor with the king, his triumph was short lived because William died in 1702. Soon afterward, Defoe's enemies had him arrested and imprisoned for a short time. For the next seventeen years, much of Defoe's writing dealt with politics. It was primarily of a <u>satirical</u> nature and was intended to bring attention to the issues of the day.

From 1719 to 1724 was undoubtedly the greatest period of Defoe's literary career. During that relatively short five-year period, he published nine novels, several of which have become classics of English literature. The most famous of those works is *Robinson Crusoe* (1719), which tells the story of the <u>eponymous</u> shipwrecked castaway. While his source of inspiration for the story remains a topic of controversy, most literary historians agree that Defoe based the novel on the widely known adventures of a sailor named Alexander Selkirk. *Robinson Crusoe* is often regarded as Defoe's attempt to impart his ideas on cultural imperialism. The European Crusoe turns his tropical island prison into a colony, and he becomes the natural ruler of the people he encounters. *Robinson Crusoe* was an immediate hit, selling out four printings in a single year, and it has since become one of the most widely published novels in history. It is often called the first realistic fiction novel and has been credited with starting the adventure story genre of literature.

Following the success of *Robinson Crusoe*, Defoe wrote and published two more stories related to the island adventurer, yet neither was as successful as the first. His next great achievement came in 1722

with *A Journal of the Plague Year*, which highlighted the events of the Great Plague of London in 1665. The novel is so realistic that it reads like an accurate historical account of the events. Defoe is believed to have relied upon his uncle's diary as the major source of factual information for the novel. So true to the events of the plague is the work that it is often not considered a book of fiction, but it is instead regarded as nonfiction.

The same year that *A Journal of the Plague Year* was published, Defoe also published *Moll Flanders*, a fictional work about an immoral woman's criminal life. In the story, Moll Flanders cons her way through several adventures while having many husbands and children in her search for riches and happiness. After publishing a couple more novels, Defoe returned mainly to writing nonfiction works before his death from a stroke in 1731. Altogether, he penned more than 500 pamphlets, essays, articles, and books and is considered the father of modern journalism and the realistic novel.

*Glossary

satirical: relating to the use of irony, sarcasm, or ridicule
eponymous: giving one's name to a title, group, city, or something similar

11 According to paragraph 1, which of the following is true about Daniel Defoe?

   (A) He was widely recognized as a great writer only after he died.

   (B) He was harmed by the fact that he often had little or no money.

   (C) He preferred to engage in business activities than political ones.

   (D) He lived nearly his entire life in the city of London, England.

Paragraph 1 is marked with an arrow (➡).

12 In paragraph 1, all of the following questions are answered EXCEPT:

   (A) How well was Daniel Defoe paid for the works that he produced?

   (B) What is Daniel Defoe's contribution to writing considered to be?

   (C) What were some of the works that helped Daniel Defoe achieve fame?

   (D) What kind of personal life did Daniel Defoe have?

Paragraph 1 is marked with an arrow (➡).

Daniel Defoe and His Writings

➡ One of the founders of both modern English journalism and literature is English writer Daniel Defoe. While primarily known for being a journalist and pamphleteer in his early years, he later attained fame for his novels, particularly *Robinson Crusoe*, *A Journal of the Plague Year*, and *Moll Flanders*. Born to an affluent family of candle merchants in London, England, in 1660, Defoe finished his education and went into business dealing commodities such as wool and wine. Despite some business success, Defoe was plagued with debt issues for practically his entire life, which had a deleterious effect on him, his wife, and his eight children. While he engaged in business for decades, he considered himself a writer and political activist rather than a businessman.

More Available ▲

13 The author discusses "the Glorious Revolution" in order to

(A) explain the historical context that led to the revolution taking place

(B) express disagreement with the results of the revolution on England

(C) point out that Daniel Defoe nearly lost his life due to the events of the revolution

(D) describe how the events of the revolution pertained to Daniel Defoe's life

14 According to paragraph 2, Daniel Defoe wrote *A True-Born Englishman* because

(A) he believed that there were too many foreigners living in England

(B) he was defending the king of England against racially prejudiced charges

(C) he had a desire to earn the king's favor to help his financial situation

(D) he wanted to express the importance of race in English politics

Paragraph 2 is marked with an arrow (➡).

➡ Many of Defoe's early writings dealt with the political and social issues of his time. The most prominent of these was the Glorious Revolution of 1688, which toppled King James II from the English throne. As a result of the revolution, William of Orange, the ruler of the Netherlands and husband of James's daughter Mary, became the king of England. A staunch defender of the revolution, Defoe wrote several pamphlets defending William's right to rule. His most famous one, entitled *A True-Born Englishman*, was printed in 1701 and defended the king against racial attacks by his enemies. They claimed the king had no right to rule because he was Dutch and, accordingly, not a true Englishman. Defoe's pamphlet challenged the English people's belief that they were a pure race by pointing out that they were descended from many foreign tribes. Although his writing won Defoe favor with the king, his triumph was short lived because William died in 1702. Soon afterward, Defoe's enemies had him arrested and imprisoned for a short time. For the next seventeen years, much of Defoe's writing dealt with politics. It was primarily of a satirical nature and was intended to bring attention to the issues of the day.

*Glossary

satirical: relating to the use of irony, sarcasm, or ridicule

15 The word "impart" in the passage is closest in meaning to

(A) communicate

(B) resolve

(C) simplify

(D) illuminate

From 1719 to 1724 was undoubtedly the greatest period of Defoe's literary career. During that relatively short five-year period, he published nine novels, several of which have become classics of English literature. The most famous of those works is *Robinson Crusoe* (1719), which tells the story of the eponymous shipwrecked castaway. While his source of inspiration for the story remains a topic of controversy, most literary historians agree that Defoe based the novel on the widely known adventures of a sailor named Alexander Selkirk. *Robinson Crusoe* is often regarded as Defoe's attempt to impart his ideas on cultural imperialism. The European Crusoe turns his tropical island prison into a colony, and he becomes the natural ruler of the people he encounters. *Robinson Crusoe* was an immediate hit, selling out four printings in a single year, and it has since become one of the most widely published novels in history. It is often called the first realistic fiction novel and has been credited with starting the adventure story genre of literature.

*Glossary

eponymous: giving one's name to a title, group, city, or something similar

16 According to paragraph 4, *A Journal of the Plague Year* is often considered a nonfiction book because

(A) Daniel Defoe made sure that he used multiple sources when writing the work

(B) the book contained testimonies by people who had lived through the plague year

(C) the accuracy of the novel makes it read like it is an historical account

(D) Daniel Defoe's uncle, whose diary inspired the book, was a plague survivor

Paragraph 4 is marked with an arrow (➡).

17 The word "penned" in the passage is closest in meaning to

(A) published

(B) sold

(C) wrote

(D) designed

18 In paragraph 5, the author of the passage implies that the character Moll Flanders

(A) is unconcerned with how she breaks the law in the novel

(B) lives in and travels on several continents during the story

(C) is one of the most inspiring female protagonists in literature

(D) is based on a woman that Daniel Defoe was acquainted with

Paragraph 5 is marked with an arrow (⇨).

➡ Following the success of *Robinson Crusoe*, Defoe wrote and published two more stories related to the island adventurer, yet neither was as successful as the first. His next great achievement came in 1722 with *A Journal of the Plague Year*, which highlighted the events of the Great Plague of London in 1665. The novel is so realistic that it reads like an accurate historical account of the events. Defoe is believed to have relied upon his uncle's diary as the major source of factual information for the novel. So true to the events of the plague is the work that it is often not considered a book of fiction, but it is instead regarded as nonfiction.

⇨ The same year that *A Journal of the Plague Year* was published, Defoe also published *Moll Flanders*, a fictional work about an immoral woman's criminal life. In the story, Moll Flanders cons her way through several adventures while having many husbands and children in her search for riches and happiness. After publishing a couple more novels, Defoe returned mainly to writing nonfiction works before his death from a stroke in 1731. Altogether, he penned more than 500 pamphlets, essays, articles, and books and is considered the father of modern journalism and the realistic novel.

19 Look at the four squares [■] that indicate where the following sentence could be added to the passage.

A real person, he had lived the life of a privateer until he was stranded on an uninhabited island in the Pacific Ocean for more than four years.

Where would the sentence best fit?

Click on a square [■] to add the sentence to the passage.

From 1719 to 1724 was undoubtedly the greatest period of Defoe's literary career. During that relatively short five-year period, he published nine novels, several of which have become classics of English literature. The most famous of those works is *Robinson Crusoe* (1719), which tells the story of the eponymous shipwrecked castaway. While his source of inspiration for the story remains a topic of controversy, most literary historians agree that Defoe based the novel on the widely known adventures of a sailor named Alexander Selkirk. **1** *Robinson Crusoe* is often regarded as Defoe's attempt to impart his ideas on cultural imperialism. **2** The European Crusoe turns his tropical island prison into a colony, and he becomes the natural ruler of the people he encounters. **3** *Robinson Crusoe* was an immediate hit, selling out four printings in a single year, and it has since become one of the most widely published novels in history. **4** It is often called the first realistic fiction novel and has been credited with starting the adventure story genre of literature.

*Glossary

eponymous: giving one's name to a title, group, city, or something similar

20 **Directions:** An introductory sentence for a brief summary of the passage is provided below. Complete the summary by selecting the THREE answer choices that express the most important ideas of the passage. Some sentences do not belong because they express ideas that are not presented in the passage or are minor ideas in the passage. **This question is worth 2 points.**

Drag your answer choices to the spaces where they belong. To remove an answer choice, click on it. To review the passage, click on **VIEW TEXT**.

Daniel Defoe was a journalist and political writer, but he is more famous for several of the novels that he authored.

-
-
-

ANSWER CHOICES

1 Daniel Defoe wrote political treatises both when he was starting out as a writer and also at the end of his life.

2 At one point in his life, Daniel Defoe was arrested by supporters of the king and spent some time being imprisoned.

3 Daniel Defoe had a very large family, and that fact often caused him to suffer financially all throughout his life.

4 Many of the characters that Daniel Defoe wrote about in his novels were based upon people that he personally knew.

5 *Robinson Crusoe* is the best-known novel of all of the works Daniel Defoe wrote during a five-year period.

6 *A Journal of the Plague Year* and *Moll Flanders* were two novels that brought Daniel Defoe to the attention of many people.

Art Conservation Methods

There are several subdivisions of art, among them being painting, sculpture, drawing, and etching. While each genre features a wide variety of differences, they all share one similarity: Over time, every work of art both ages and depreciates. The manner in which the condition of a piece of art decreases depends upon the care taken to preserve it. There are numerous ways to conserve paintings and other works, including state-of-the-art methods and ones that have been utilized for centuries.

Aside from fire, water exposure, and rips, tears, and other damage caused by destructive forces, artwork can deteriorate due to subtler and slower-acting causes. The most important factor affecting how well a piece of art is preserved is the quality of the air surrounding it. If an artwork is stored or displayed in a location with a great amount of dust or high humidity or if there are dramatic changes in temperature from hot to cold or the reverse, then there will be an adverse effect on it. Paintings, etchings, and drawings, for example, are normally framed in wood, which expands and retracts at varying rates depending on the temperature and humidity. This places stress on the frame, which can result in the wood warping and splitting. Furthermore, the canvas a painting is created on may warp and buckle while oil paints may crack or flake off if the air is too damp or too dry. Additionally, artwork exposed to soot, dust, dirt, and other forms of grime may become so coated with them that its colors become dull or get obscured to some extent.

The first step to preserving works of art is prevention. Modern temperature- and humidity-controlled display cases are the norm in well-funded galleries. Proper care in the handling and storing of artwork also considerably helps preserve it. Unfortunately, for many pieces, it is too late as they have already suffered damage, so in these instances, it is necessary to find an expert in conservation. This person, called an art restorer, first carefully examines the work to assess the amount of damage by employing not only the naked eye but also sophisticated cameras, X-rays, and laser equipment. Once the damage has been

determined, the actual restoration work can begin. During the entire process, the restorer documents every step by taking photographs, making video recordings of the restoration, and creating paper records to ensure the owner of the artwork that care has been taken with the restoration.

Typically, the initial act of any restoration is to clean the piece. When the item is a fresco, mural, or large sculpture, this is done on site, but the process of cleaning is almost always performed in the restorer's workshop when the artwork is a painting. With paintings, the canvas is first removed from the frame and then stretched out. Next, the restorer carefully cleans the painting with soft, wet cotton swabs by using <u>saliva</u>. Saliva has better properties for such work than water does since it is more viscous and therefore does not seep into the cracks in the painting. The damp cotton swabs effectively collect grime and remove it from the paint. In the past, art restorers employed a variety of materials, including beer, raw potatoes, bread, and wood ash, to remove grime from paintings. In fact, on one occasion, bread was used to clean Michelangelo's frescoes in the Sistine Chapel in the Vatican.

Depending upon the size of the work and the amount of impurities on it, cleaning the piece may require several hours or days of exacting work. Once that task is complete, the restorer must repair any rents in the canvas, which is usually accomplished by repairing it from the back. Patches are placed over holes and glued on while paintings done on linen may have them sewn on the back. A second layer of canvas or wood is sometimes added to the back to provide more support. Following that, the restorer begins the painstaking process of adding paint to where the work has incurred damage. This act, called inpainting, must be done in the same style as the original to be as invisible as possible. Once the inpainting is finished, the painting is returned to its frame and is once again ready for display.

*Glossary

buckle: to bend or curl, often as a result of heat or pressure
saliva: watery fluid that is secreted in the mouth; spit

Beginning

Art Conservation Methods

➡ There are several subdivisions of art, among them being painting, sculpture, drawing, and etching. While each genre features a wide variety of differences, they all share one similarity: Over time, every work of art both ages and depreciates. The manner in which the condition of a piece of art decreases depends upon the care taken to preserve it. There are numerous ways to conserve paintings and other works, including state-of-the-art methods and ones that have been utilized for centuries.

⇨ Aside from fire, water exposure, and rips, tears, and other damage caused by destructive forces, artwork can deteriorate due to subtler and slower-acting causes. The most important factor affecting how well a piece of art is preserved is the quality of the air surrounding it. If an artwork is stored or displayed in a location with a great amount of dust or high humidity or if there are dramatic changes in temperature from hot to cold or the reverse, then there will be an adverse effect on it. Paintings, etchings, and drawings, for example, are normally framed in wood, which expands and retracts at varying rates depending on the temperature and humidity. This places stress on the frame, which can result in the wood warping and splitting. Furthermore, the canvas a painting is created on may warp and buckle while oil paints may crack or flake off if the air is too damp or too dry. Additionally, artwork exposed to soot, dust, dirt, and other forms of grime may become so coated with them that its colors become dull or get obscured to some extent.

21 In paragraph 1, the author implies that artwork

Ⓐ can have its condition decrease slowly if good care is taken of it

Ⓑ can be preserved so well that it does not depreciate at all

Ⓒ should rely on modern preservation methods rather than traditional ones

Ⓓ should be allowed to have its condition get worse for the sake of realism

Paragraph 1 is marked with an arrow (➡).

22 The word "deteriorate" in the passage is closest in meaning to

Ⓐ erode

Ⓑ recede

Ⓒ worsen

Ⓓ dismiss

23 According to paragraph 2, which of the following is NOT true about how air can affect artwork?

Ⓐ Air that contains a great deal of dirt in it may result in paintings losing their vivid colors.

Ⓑ Both dry and moist air can cause oil paints to crack or come off the paintings they are on.

Ⓒ Air that is too hot or cold for long periods of time can cause canvases to develop cracks.

Ⓓ The temperature of the air can cause the frames paintings are in to become damaged.

Paragraph 2 is marked with an arrow (⇨).

*Glossary

buckle: to bend or curl, often as a result of heat or pressure

More Available

24 In paragraph 3, the author uses "sophisticated cameras, X-rays, and laser equipment" as examples of

   (A) equipment that works better than the naked eye at determining the value of art

   (B) modern-day tools that are the preferred equipment of the majority of art restorers

   (C) tools that can be utilized by art restorers to find out what is wrong with artwork

   (D) some of the tools that people in the past were unable to use while restoring damaged art

Paragraph 3 is marked with an arrow (➡).

25 According to paragraph 3, which of the following is true about art restorers?

   (A) They are usually talented artists themselves, which lets them restore art well.

   (B) They take extensive effort to record all of the work they do on pieces of art.

   (C) Many of them work at art galleries while others have their own studios to work in.

   (D) They prefer recording their actions with video cameras to creating paperwork.

Paragraph 3 is marked with an arrow (➡).

➡ The first step to preserving works of art is prevention. Modern temperature- and humidity-controlled display cases are the norm in well-funded galleries. Proper care in the handling and storing of artwork also considerably helps preserve it. Unfortunately, for many pieces, it is too late as they have already suffered damage, so in these instances, it is necessary to find an expert in conservation. This person, called an art restorer, first carefully examines the work to assess the amount of damage by employing not only the naked eye but also sophisticated cameras, X-rays, and laser equipment. Once the damage has been determined, the actual restoration work can begin. During the entire process, the restorer documents every step by taking photographs, making video recordings of the restoration, and creating paper records to ensure the owner of the artwork that care has been taken with the restoration.

26 The word "this" in the passage refers to

(A) any restoration

(B) the item

(C) a fresco, mural, or large sculpture

(D) the process of cleaning

27 Which of the following can be inferred from paragraph 4 about the materials used to clean artwork?

(A) A wide variety of items from the natural world are effective cleaners.

(B) It took many years of experimentation to determine which ones work the best.

(C) Most of the materials are equivalent to one another in their effectiveness.

(D) The majority of the materials must be mixed with water to work well.

Paragraph 4 is marked with an arrow (➡).

➡ Typically, the initial act of any restoration is to clean the piece. When the item is a fresco, mural, or large sculpture, this is done on site, but the process of cleaning is almost always performed in the restorer's workshop when the artwork is a painting. With paintings, the canvas is first removed from the frame and then stretched out. Next, the restorer carefully cleans the painting with soft, wet cotton swabs by using saliva. Saliva has better properties for such work than water does since it is more viscous and therefore does not seep into the cracks in the painting. The damp cotton swabs effectively collect grime and remove it from the paint. In the past, art restorers employed a variety of materials, including beer, raw potatoes, bread, and wood ash, to remove grime from paintings. In fact, on one occasion, bread was used to clean Michelangelo's frescoes in the Sistine Chapel in the Vatican.

*Glossary

saliva: watery fluid that is secreted in the mouth; spit

End

28 The word "Patches" in the passage is closest in meaning to

(A) Strings

(B) Covers

(C) Boards

(D) Holes

Depending upon the size of the work and the amount of impurities on it, cleaning the piece may require several hours or days of exacting work. Once that task is complete, the restorer must repair any rents in the canvas, which is usually accomplished by repairing it from the back. Patches are placed over holes and glued on while paintings done on linen may have them sewn on the back. A second layer of canvas or wood is sometimes added to the back to provide more support. Following that, the restorer begins the painstaking process of adding paint to where the work has incurred damage. This act, called inpainting, must be done in the same style as the original to be as invisible as possible. Once the inpainting is finished, the painting is returned to its frame and is once again ready for display.

29 Look at the four squares [■] that indicate where the following sentence could be added to the passage.

Many restorers specialize in the art of a specific period rather than repair works from different times that used various painting methods.

Where would the sentence best fit?

Click on a square [■] to add the sentence to the passage.

Depending upon the size of the work and the amount of impurities on it, cleaning the piece may require several hours or days of exacting work. Once that task is complete, the restorer must repair any rents in the canvas, which is usually accomplished by repairing it from the back. Patches are placed over holes and glued on while paintings done on linen may have them sewn on the back. ■ A second layer of canvas or wood is sometimes added to the back to provide more support. ■ Following that, the restorer begins the painstaking process of adding paint to where the work has incurred damage. ■ This act, called inpainting, must be done in the same style as the original to be as invisible as possible. ■ Once the inpainting is finished, the painting is returned to its frame and is once again ready for display.

30 Directions: Select the appropriate statements from the answer choices and match them to the type of art conservation to which they relate. TWO of the answer choices will NOT be used. **This question is worth 3 points.**

Drag your answer choices to the spaces where they belong. To remove an answer choice, click on it. To review the passage, click on **VIEW TEXT**.

ANSWER CHOICES

1. Employs inpainting to fix parts of a painting that have been damaged

2. Uses special paints that are designed not to break down over time

3. Keeps the works of art in special cases to monitor their exposure to air

4. Utilizes saliva to remove grime and other impurities from a work of art

5. Handles the artwork in a manner that does not cause damage to it

6. Bans the taking of pictures of artwork that may be sensitive to flashes

7. Fixes various rips or tears that may exist in the canvas by patching them

TYPE OF ART CONSERVATION

Restoration (Select 3)

-
-
-

Prevention (Select 2)

-
-

Actual Test

03

Reading Section Directions

This section measures your ability to understand academic passages in English. You will have **54 minutes** to read and answer questions about **3 passages**. A clock at the top of the screen will show you how much time is remaining.

Most questions are worth 1 point but the last question for each passage is worth more than 1 point. The directions for the last question indicate how many points you may receive.

Some passages include a word or phrase that is <u>underlined</u>. Click on the word or phrase to see a definition or an explanation.

When you want to move to the next question, click on **NEXT**. You may skip questions and go back to them later. If you want to return to previous questions, click on **BACK**. You can click on **REVIEW** at any time, and the review screen will show you which questions you have answered and which you have not answered. From this review screen, you may go directly to any question you have already seen in the Reading section.

Click on **CONTINUE** to go on.

The Dingo

The dingo is a type of wild canine that lives primarily in Australia and is believed to have evolved from a species of domesticated dog that migrated there from East Asia approximately 4,000 years in the past. The dingo has a wide range of habitats as it lives both in the tropical rainforests in the north and in the large tracts of deserts and dry grasslands that comprise the Australian interior, which is called the Outback. Considered a pest by most Australians, great efforts have been taken to keeping it away from the populated coastal regions. Nevertheless, despite numerous human efforts to reduce its numbers, the dingo still thrives.

The dingo has a similar size and body shape as its dog cousins. Most dingoes are orange-brown in color but have black coloring around the nose and ears and sometimes have light coloring on their lower bodies and lower legs. The dingo has a pointed snout, ears that stand up, and a long tail. While males tend to be larger than females, an adult dingo is typically about a meter and a half in length and half a meter in height while weighing anywhere between twelve and twenty kilograms. Dingoes communicate with one another through a complex system of howls, barks, and growls that zoologists do not fully understand.

Breeding once a year each spring, a female dingo has a gestation period lasting slightly more than two months, whereupon she then produces a litter averaging five pups but containing up to ten of them. The pups remain in an underground den for the first month of their lives, stay with their parents for eight to ten months after birth, and subsequently disperse to new regions when the next year's mating season begins. At first, young dingoes wander and hunt alone, but they eventually form mating pairs and live together to raise their pups. Occasionally, several generations of dingoes reside together, form a pack of up to a dozen animals, and have a territory that they control. This territory is loosely defined though, and its boundaries may shift if the food supply is inadequate.

Despite the dingo's average size, there is no larger land-dwelling predator on the entire continent. It tends to hunt during the cooler parts of the day around dawn and toward dusk and may hunt alone or in packs. Solitary hunters chase and kill small game such as birds, rabbits, and lizards whereas packs hunt large game and may kill cattle, kangaroos, and even huge water buffaloes. The dingo is known to consume fish, fruit and other plants, and sometimes insects and will also eat dead animals if it comes across them. Those dingoes residing near towns and cities scavenge garbage dumps for discarded human food.

With regard to its relations with humans, the dingo has something of a mixed history. The Aborigines, who are the native inhabitants of Australia, venerate the dingo as it is a major part of their folklore. Images of the dingo frequently appear in both cave and rock paintings, and the Aborigines additionally tell a number of myths related to the animal. In their stories, the Aborigines regard the dingo as a combination of good and evil as the animal is considered both a protector and force of misfortune yet sometimes even an omen of death. In some tales, dingoes are depicted as mischievous tricksters that employ their powers to deceive humans.

On the other hand, modern-day Australians, many of whom descend from European settlers, frequently have a strong dislike for the animal. Ranchers consider the dingo a threat to their livestock herds, and laws permit them to kill any dingoes that encroach upon their property or that attack their herds. In the 1920s, a massive fence—the Dingo Fence—was erected at great effort and expense to keep dingoes out of the southeast region of the country, where the majority of Australia's population lives. Yet it seems that the primary threat to the dingo is its own breeding practices. In recent years, many dingoes have been interbreeding with domestic dogs, so new generations of dingoes have gradually been losing the wild instincts that have permitted them to survive in the harsh lands of Australia for so long.

*Glossary

gestation period: the time that a female carries her baby or babies in her womb
Aborigine: one of the native people of Australia

Beginning ▲

1　Which of the sentences below best expresses the essential information in the highlighted sentence in the passage? Incorrect answer choices change the meaning in important ways or leave out essential information.

The dingo has a wide range of habitats as it lives both in the tropical rainforests in the north and in the large tracts of deserts and dry grasslands that comprise the Australian interior, which is called the Outback.

Ⓐ There are some dingoes that wander from Australia's rainforests down to the Outback.

Ⓑ The dingo is capable of living in Australian ecosystems as varied as deserts, grasslands, and rainforests.

Ⓒ Most dingoes can be found in rainforests, but others also live in deserts and grasslands.

Ⓓ While most dingoes prefer to live in the Outback, some are also found living in deserts and rainforests.

The Dingo

The dingo is a type of wild canine that lives primarily in Australia and is believed to have evolved from a species of domesticated dog that migrated there from East Asia approximately 4,000 years in the past. The dingo has a wide range of habitats as it lives both in the tropical rainforests in the north and in the large tracts of deserts and dry grasslands that comprise the Australian interior, which is called the Outback. Considered a pest by most Australians, great efforts have been taken to keeping it away from the populated coastal regions. Nevertheless, despite numerous human efforts to reduce its numbers, the dingo still thrives.

2   According to paragraph 2, which of the
following is NOT true about the dingo?

(A) Adult females are usually smaller in size
than adult males.

(B) The dingo vocalizes sounds in a number
of ways to communicate.

(C) It tends to have different colors on various
parts of its body.

(D) Its snout can be pointed and long
whereas its tail is fairly short.

Paragraph 2 is marked with an arrow (➡).

3   According to paragraph 3, dingo packs may
claim new territory because

(A) they are trying to expand the area of land
that they control

(B) they are looking to increase the amount of
food they have access to

(C) they defeat a rival pack and then take
over the territory it had controlled

(D) they need to have a safe place to give
birth to their pups

Paragraph 3 is marked with an arrow (⇨).

➡ The dingo has a similar size and body shape
as its dog cousins. Most dingoes are orange-brown
in color but have black coloring around the nose
and ears and sometimes have light coloring on
their lower bodies and lower legs. The dingo has a
pointed snout, ears that stand up, and a long tail.
While males tend to be larger than females, an adult
dingo is typically about a meter and a half in length
and half a meter in height while weighing anywhere
between twelve and twenty kilograms. Dingoes
communicate with one another through a complex
system of howls, barks, and growls that zoologists
do not fully understand.

⇨ Breeding once a year each spring, a female
dingo has a gestation period lasting slightly more
than two months, whereupon she then produces a
litter averaging five pups but containing up to ten of
them. The pups remain in an underground den for
the first month of their lives, stay with their parents
for eight to ten months after birth, and subsequently
disperse to new regions when the next year's
mating season begins. At first, young dingoes
wander and hunt alone, but they eventually form
mating pairs and live together to raise their pups.
Occasionally, several generations of dingoes reside
together, form a pack of up to a dozen animals, and
have a territory that they control. This territory is
loosely defined though, and its boundaries may shift
if the food supply is inadequate.

*Glossary

gestation period: the time that a female carries her baby or
babies in her womb

4 Which of the following can be inferred from paragraph 4 about dingo packs?

(A) The dingoes comprising them work together effectively when they hunt.

(B) Most of them hunt during the daylight hours when other animals are sleeping.

(C) They have been known to attack humans when food is in short supply.

(D) Some of them can cover a vast amount of territory while hunting in a single day.

Paragraph 4 is marked with an arrow (➡).

5 In stating that the Aborigines "venerate the dingo," the author means that the Aborigines

(A) are afraid of the dingo

(B) hunt the dingo

(C) revere the dingo

(D) avoid the dingo

6 According to paragraph 5, which of the following is true about how the Aborigines think of the dingo?

(A) They consider it to be cleverer and more intelligent than many humans are.

(B) They respect the dingo for its ability to survive in the harsh Outback.

(C) They recognize both its good and bad aspects and tell many tales about it.

(D) They regard it positively since they sometimes tamed dingoes in the past.

Paragraph 5 is marked with an arrow (⇨).

➡ Despite the dingo's average size, there is no larger land-dwelling predator on the entire continent. It tends to hunt during the cooler parts of the day around dawn and toward dusk and may hunt alone or in packs. Solitary hunters chase and kill small game such as birds, rabbits, and lizards whereas packs hunt large game and may kill cattle, kangaroos, and even huge water buffaloes. The dingo is known to consume fish, fruit and other plants, and sometimes insects and will also eat dead animals if it comes across them. Those dingoes residing near towns and cities scavenge garbage dumps for discarded human food.

⇨ With regard to its relations with humans, the dingo has something of a mixed history. The Aborigines, who are the native inhabitants of Australia, venerate the dingo as it is a major part of their folklore. Images of the dingo frequently appear in both cave and rock paintings, and the Aborigines additionally tell a number of myths related to the animal. In their stories, the Aborigines regard the dingo as a combination of good and evil as the animal is considered both a protector and force of misfortune yet sometimes even an omen of death. In some tales, dingoes are depicted as mischievous tricksters that employ their powers to deceive humans.

*Glossary

Aborigine: one of the native people of Australia

7   The phrase "encroach upon" in the passage is closest in meaning to

Ⓐ threaten

Ⓑ move toward

Ⓒ trespass on

Ⓓ live near

8   According to paragraph 6, the dingo presently faces the greatest amount of danger from

Ⓐ ranchers who shoot the animal when it threatens their herds

Ⓑ breeding with other animals, which makes it lose its wildness

Ⓒ people who set traps for dingoes in order to kill them

Ⓓ Aborigines who enjoy hunting the dingo for sport and food

Paragraph 6 is marked with an arrow (➡).

➡ On the other hand, modern-day Australians, many of whom descend from European settlers, frequently have a strong dislike for the animal. Ranchers consider the dingo a threat to their livestock herds, and laws permit them to kill any dingoes that encroach upon their property or that attack their herds. In the 1920s, a massive fence—the Dingo Fence—was erected at great effort and expense to keep dingoes out of the southeast region of the country, where the majority of Australia's population lives. Yet it seems that the primary threat to the dingo is its own breeding practices. In recent years, many dingoes have been interbreeding with domestic dogs, so new generations of dingoes have gradually been losing the wild instincts that have permitted them to survive in the harsh lands of Australia for so long.

9   Look at the four squares [■] that indicate where the following sentence could be added to the passage.

This makes the dingo an apex predator as, other than humans, the only animals on land that it needs to fear are the myriad poisonous snakes that dwell in Australia.

Where would the sentence best fit?

Click on a square [■] to add the sentence to the passage.

Despite the dingo's average size, there is no larger land-dwelling predator on the entire continent. **1** It tends to hunt during the cooler parts of the day around dawn and toward dusk and may hunt alone or in packs. **2** Solitary hunters chase and kill small game such as birds, rabbits, and lizards whereas packs hunt large game and may kill cattle, kangaroos, and even huge water buffaloes. **3** The dingo is known to consume fish, fruit and other plants, and sometimes insects and will also eat dead animals if it comes across them. **4** Those dingoes residing near towns and cities scavenge garbage dumps for discarded human food.

10 **Directions:** An introductory sentence for a brief summary of the passage is provided below. Complete the summary by selecting the THREE answer choices that express the most important ideas of the passage. Some sentences do not belong because they express ideas that are not presented in the passage or are minor ideas in the passage. **This question is worth 2 points.**

Drag your answer choices to the spaces where they belong. To remove an answer choice, click on it. To review the passage, click on **VIEW TEXT**.

The dingo is a wild dog that resides in various ecosystems in Australia, but it is considered a nuisance by many Australians.

-
-
-

ANSWER CHOICES

1 Australian ranchers dislike the dingo since it hunts their animals, so they often kill dingoes that harm their livestock.

2 Dingo pups stay in their dens for one month and remain with their parents for nearly a year after being born.

3 The dingo is capable of living in the Australian Outback, which is mostly desert, but it can also survive in rainforests.

4 Female dingoes tend to be much larger than males, which can weigh up to twenty kilograms and be 1.5 meters in length.

5 The Aborigines tell many stories about the dingo and consider it a trickster in some of their myths.

6 Dingoes often live and hunt together in packs, which enables them to kill animals much larger than themselves.

The Tigris-Euphrates Marshlands

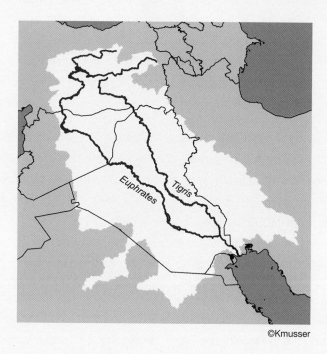

©Kmusser

The land around the Tigris and Euphrates rivers was the cradle of one of the world's first civilizations, called Mesopotamia, which existed in the land that is modern-day Iraq. The two great rivers start as small tributaries in the highlands of Turkey, move through Syria, and then flow through Iraq for much of their length. Near the Iraqi city of Qurna, the Euphrates unites with the Tigris, so the two become a single river called Shatt al-Arab, and it takes their combined flow to the Persian Gulf. Near the confluence of the rivers are several marshlands that combine to form an ecosystem that has several unique species and additionally serves as a wintering place for many species of birds living in Eurasia. In recent years, the entire region has undergone numerous changes on account of war and draining projects that presently threaten the fragile ecosystem.

The region is not one vast swamp but is instead a system of rivers, streams, canals, and separate marshlands. Altogether, the wetlands cover approximately 35,000 square kilometers. The largest is the Hawizeh Marsh, which is located along the border of Iraq and Iran. It is west of the Tigris River and east of Qurna. The second largest marsh is the Amarah Marsh, which is found between the Tigris and Euphrates rivers slightly east of where they link at Qurna. A smaller marsh—the Hammar Marsh—lies west of the city of Basra and was once adjacent to a large lake, Lake Hammar.

These marshes are noted for the large numbers of waterfowl and several mammalian species residing there. Among the birds are the Iraq babbler, Basra reed-warbler, Dalmatian pelican, pygmy

cormorant, imperial eagle, white-tailed eagle, and marbled duck. The majority of these species only winter in the marshlands after flying great distances from northern lands in Eurasia. As such, the marshes are crucial to these birds' life cycles. Ornithologists have additionally determined that the marshlands are the only breeding grounds for the Iraq babbler and Basra reed-warbler, so it is vital to them that the marshlands do not vanish. There are also some mammals, such as Bunn's short-tailed bandicoot rat and the Mesopotamian gerbil, that only live in the marshlands. They are the homes of numerous Asian water buffaloes, which the people of the region rely upon as the mainstays of their animal herds, as well.

The people living around the marshlands were at the center of a great amount of conflict in the late twentieth century and early twenty-first century. During the Iran-Iraq War (1980-1988), the region on the border of the two countries was the scene of several protracted battles, so both the people and the wildlife in the region suffered considerably. After the Gulf War (1990-1991), the Shia Muslims living in the region rose up in rebellion against the Iraqi government but were ruthlessly put down. As further punishment, extensive draining of the marshlands, particularly the centralized Amarah Marsh, Lake Hammar, and Hammar Marsh, took place. The waters in these areas were redirected to other regions and used for irrigation. The end result was that a great amount of marshland was suddenly transformed into desert.

Following the end of Saddam Hussein's regime in 2003, the draining of the marshlands was halted. By 2006, some life had returned to the region as it began recovering. This was assisted by record snowfalls in Turkey in 2005 and 2006, which resulted in a large volume of snowmelt in the Tigris and Euphrates. This additional water helped restore roughly forty percent of the drained marshes to their previous states. That, in turn, led to the return of some wildlife, which had abandoned the region when the marshlands were drained.

Exactly how extensive the damage done to the land and wildlife is uncertain today, but studies are being conducted to determine that. While the central Amarah and Hammar marshes were almost completely drained, the Hawizeh Marsh on the border with Iran did not suffer as much harm. The Iranian side of the marsh is extensively protected and serves as a major breeding ground for numerous species of birds. Presently, it appears there is some hope for the complete restoration of the marshes, which will accordingly result in the preservation of the birds and mammals residing in them.

*Glossary

highland: a plateau; a piece of land that is elevated above the land around it

ornithologist: a scientist who studies birds

The Tigris-Euphrates Marshlands

The land around the Tigris and Euphrates rivers was the cradle of one of the world's first civilizations, called Mesopotamia, which existed in the land that is modern-day Iraq. The two great rivers start as small tributaries in the highlands of Turkey, move through Syria, and then flow through Iraq for much of their length. Near the Iraqi city of Qurna, the Euphrates unites with the Tigris, so the two become a single river called Shatt al-Arab, and it takes their combined flow to the Persian Gulf. Near the confluence of the rivers are several marshlands that combine to form an ecosystem that has several unique species and additionally serves as a wintering place for many species of birds living in Eurasia. In recent years, the entire region has undergone numerous changes on account of war and draining projects that presently threaten the fragile ecosystem.

➡ The region is not one vast swamp but is instead a system of rivers, streams, canals, and separate marshlands. Altogether, the wetlands cover approximately 35,000 square kilometers. The largest is the Hawizeh Marsh, which is located along the border of Iraq and Iran. It is west of the Tigris River and east of Qurna. The second largest marsh is the Amarah Marsh, which is found between the Tigris and Euphrates rivers slightly east of where they link at Qurna. A smaller marsh—the Hammar Marsh— lies west of the city of Basra and was once adjacent to a large lake, Lake Hammar.

11 The word "confluence" in the passage is closest in meaning to

- Ⓐ source
- Ⓑ headwaters
- Ⓒ union
- Ⓓ delta

12 The author discusses "the Hawizeh Marsh" in order to

- Ⓐ point out both its size and its precise location
- Ⓑ describe some of the species living in it
- Ⓒ contrast how it is different from the Hammar Marsh
- Ⓓ discuss its relevance to Lake Hammar

13 In paragraph 2, which of the following can be inferred about the Hammar Marsh?

- Ⓐ It is the largest freshwater lake in all of Iraq.
- Ⓑ It provides drinking water for the residents of Basra.
- Ⓒ It has become smaller in size over the years.
- Ⓓ It has streams that drain into the Tigris and Euphrates rivers.

Paragraph 2 is marked with an arrow (➡).

*Glossary

highland: a plateau; a piece of land that is elevated above the land around it

14 In paragraph 3, the author's description of the animals living in the marshlands mentions all of the following EXCEPT:

(A) the numbers of birds and mammals that winter in the marshlands

(B) the names of some animals that only reside in the marshlands

(C) some of the birds that use the marshlands in order to reproduce

(D) the period when many of the birds can be found in the marshlands

Paragraph 3 is marked with an arrow (➡).

15 The word "protracted" in the passage is closest in meaning to

(A) bloody

(B) horrific

(C) extended

(D) complicated

➡ These marshes are noted for the large numbers of waterfowl and several mammalian species residing there. Among the birds are the Iraq babbler, Basra reed-warbler, Dalmatian pelican, pygmy cormorant, imperial eagle, white-tailed eagle, and marbled duck. The majority of these species only winter in the marshlands after flying great distances from northern lands in Eurasia. As such, the marshes are crucial to these birds' life cycles. Ornithologists have additionally determined that the marshlands are the only breeding grounds for the Iraq babbler and Basra reed-warbler, so it is vital to them that the marshlands do not vanish. There are also some mammals, such as Bunn's short-tailed bandicoot rat and the Mesopotamian gerbil, that only live in the marshlands. They are the homes of numerous Asian water buffaloes, which the people of the region rely upon as the mainstays of their animal herds, as well.

The people living around the marshlands were at the center of a great amount of conflict in the late twentieth century and early twenty-first century. During the Iran-Iraq War (1980-1988), the region on the border of the two countries was the scene of several protracted battles, so both the people and the wildlife in the region suffered considerably. After the Gulf War (1990-1991), the Shia Muslims living in the region rose up in rebellion against the Iraqi government but were ruthlessly put down. As further punishment, extensive draining of the marshlands, particularly the centralized Amarah Marsh, Lake Hammar, and Hammar Marsh, took place. The waters in these areas were redirected to other regions and used for irrigation. The end result was that a great amount of marshland was suddenly transformed into desert.

*Glossary

ornithologist: a scientist who studies birds

16 According to paragraph 5, why did the marshlands become bigger around 2006?

(A) Water conservation efforts throughout Iraq enabled more water to flow into the marshlands.

(B) Large amounts of snow resulted in more water going into the rivers flowing into the marshes.

(C) The Iraqis ceased their efforts to use the water in the marshes for irrigation that year.

(D) Heavy rain in both Iran and Iraq contributed to an increase in the water in the marshes.

Paragraph 5 is marked with an arrow (➡).

17 The word "which" in the passage refers to

(A) the region

(B) record snowfalls

(C) Turkey

(D) 2005 and 2006

18 According to paragraph 6, the Hawizeh Marsh was damaged less than other areas because

(A) the Iraqis could more easily drain the water from other places

(B) water from the Tigris River flows directly into a large part of it

(C) a large part of it was not drained due to the fact that it is in Iran

(D) the Iraqis made an effort to protect it due to the wildlife there

Paragraph 6 is marked with an arrow (⇨).

➡ Following the end of Saddam Hussein's regime in 2003, the draining of the marshlands was halted. By 2006, some life had returned to the region as it began recovering. This was assisted by record snowfalls in Turkey in 2005 and 2006, which resulted in a large volume of snowmelt in the Tigris and Euphrates. This additional water helped restore roughly forty percent of the drained marshes to their previous states. That, in turn, led to the return of some wildlife, which had abandoned the region when the marshlands were drained.

⇨ Exactly how extensive the damage done to the land and wildlife is uncertain today, but studies are being conducted to determine that. While the central Amarah and Hammar marshes were almost completely drained, the Hawizeh Marsh on the border with Iran did not suffer as much harm. The Iranian side of the marsh is extensively protected and serves as a major breeding ground for numerous species of birds. Presently, it appears there is some hope for the complete restoration of the marshes, which will accordingly result in the preservation of the birds and mammals residing in them.

19 Look at the four squares [■] that indicate where the following sentence could be added to the passage.

As a result, the Hawizeh Marsh remained in much better condition than any of the other marshes in the region.

Where would the sentence best fit?

Click on a square [■] to add the sentence to the passage.

■ Exactly how extensive the damage done to the land and wildlife is uncertain today, but studies are being conducted to determine that. ■ While the central Amarah and Hammar marshes were almost completely drained, the Hawizeh Marsh on the border with Iran did not suffer as much harm. ■ The Iranian side of the marsh is extensively protected and serves as a major breeding ground for numerous species of birds. ■ Presently, it appears there is some hope for the complete restoration of the marshes, which will accordingly result in the preservation of the birds and mammals residing in them.

20 **Directions:** An introductory sentence for a brief summary of the passage is provided below. Complete the summary by selecting the THREE answer choices that express the most important ideas of the passage. Some sentences do not belong because they express ideas that are not presented in the passage or are minor ideas in the passage. **This question is worth 2 points.**

Drag your answer choices to the spaces where they belong. To remove an answer choice, click on it. To review the passage, click on **VIEW TEXT**.

The marshlands between the Tigris and Euphrates rivers are important ecosystems for many animals, but they have suffered great harm in recent years.

-
-
-

ANSWER CHOICES

☐1 The Tigris and Euphrates rivers flow through the Middle East and then come together to form a single river with marshlands alongside them.

☐2 Some of the marshes have increased in size recently thanks to efforts to end the draining of them.

☐3 A large number of endangered birds reproduce in the marshlands, or they spend the winter there after flying from Eurasia.

☐4 In the 1980s and 1990s, large areas in the marshlands suffered from both warfare and draining, which affected their sizes and the wildlife in them.

☐5 There are some mammals that are only found in the marshes, and other animals living there are important to the local residents.

☐6 Many of the marshes between the two rivers can be found near the cities of Basra and Qurna.

Past Attempts at Determining the Age of the Earth

By utilizing radiometric dating of rocks on the Earth and by comparing these readings to those of rocks from the moon and the oldest known meteorites, scientists have determined that the Earth is approximately 4.5 billion years old. However, it is only since the late twentieth century, when accurate dating methods were invented and lunar samples obtained by the *Apollo* missions were studied, that the figure became widely accepted. Prior to that time, calculating the age of the Earth was an inexact science resulting in widely differing opinions.

Early attempts to figure out how old the Earth is were based upon geological formations, especially the layering of rocks known as strata. Europe experienced a period of extensive canal building in the 1800s, during which time it was discovered that strata were not always neatly layered horizontally but could be tilted and misshapen in various ways. These discoveries indicated that they had been there a long time and had changed radically as they had aged. Geologists specialized in the study of strata, so they assumed the task of determining the Earth's age. In the eighteenth century, Scottish geologist James Hutton avowed that the Earth's age was without limits as it had neither a beginning nor an end. By the early nineteenth century though, many geologists disagreed with his highly unscientific conclusion that lacked concrete evidence to support it. Nevertheless, calculating the age of the Earth remained problematic for scientists because there was no precise way to utilize strata to discover its age.

One solution that was proposed suggested that scientists should avoid examining strata but instead look to the laws of thermodynamics. British scientist William Thomson (1824-1907), better known by his title, Lord Kelvin, concluded that the Earth had formed as a molten ball of rock which had a uniform temperature and which had been cooling ever since its creation. He believed that by calculating the rate of cooling to allow the Earth's rocks to solidify, the age of the Earth could be determined. He started with the premise that the Earth was 3,900 degrees Celsius at its formation. Then, Kelvin arrived at the conclusion that the Earth was somewhere between twenty and 400 million years old. The inexactness of his conclusion was the result of the unknown—at that time—exact values of geothermal gradient, which refers to how hot it gets the deeper one descends into the Earth's interior. Kelvin published his findings in 1864 and swiftly became embroiled in a decade-long controversy with geologists. Later, in the 1890s, he caused further debate by estimating that the Earth was only twenty to forty million years old.

The major problem with Kelvin's findings was that he was unaware of another heat source found in the interior of the Earth: radioactivity caused by the decay of isotopes in rocks. As a result of his ignorance, his calculations were widely inaccurate. Kelvin was additionally uninformed of the viscous nature of the planet's interior, especially the mantle, which causes wide fluctuations in the transfer of heat throughout the planet. One of Kelvin's own assistants, engineer John Perry, hypothesized that the Earth consisted of a thin layer of crust resting on top of a fluid mantle. Based upon that theory, in 1895, Perry concluded that the Earth was closer to two or three billion years old. Kelvin, however, refused to accept Perry's calculations and continued to espouse his own conclusions.

The discovery of radiation and methods to measure the radioactive decay of rocks ultimately proved both Kelvin and Perry wrong. In 1904, physicist Ernest Rutherford theorized that radioactive decay in the interior of the Earth kept replenishing the planet's heat supply, so all calculations regarding the age of the Earth based on cooling rates were therefore inaccurate. Eventually, this knowledge of radioactive decay was put to practical use when geologist Arthur Holmes created a method of dating rocks by measuring their rate of radioactive decay in 1911. Two years later in 1913, Holmes published a book entitled *The Age of the Earth*, which called for using radioactive decay as the means to measure the planet's age. Subsequent refinements of his initial work have led scientists to the conclusion that the Earth is in fact roughly 4.5 billion years old.

*Glossary

radiometric dating: a method of dating objects by analyzing the radioactive material that is in them

strata: layers of material that are piled on top of one another

Beginning ▲

21 Select the TWO answer choices from paragraph 1 that identify the methods used to identify the Earth's age that were utilized in the late 1900s. *To receive credit, you must select TWO answers.*

   (A) Dating residue from asteroids originating in deep space

   (B) Analyses of rocks that were returned from the moon

   (C) The study of various layers of ground in the Earth

   (D) The utilization of dating methods based on radioactivity

Paragraph 1 is marked with an arrow (➡).

22 Which of the following can be inferred from paragraph 1 about the age of the Earth?

   (A) There is no universally accepted way of determining it.

   (B) It has been widely known to scientists for centuries.

   (C) Many people think that the planet is only millions of years old.

   (D) Few people agreed about how old the Earth is before the 1900s.

Paragraph 1 is marked with an arrow (➡).

23 The word "assumed" in the passage is closest in meaning to

   (A) looked for

   (B) studied about

   (C) asked about

   (D) took on

Past Attempts at Determining the Age of the Earth

➡ By utilizing radiometric dating of rocks on the Earth and by comparing these readings to those of rocks from the moon and the oldest known meteorites, scientists have determined that the Earth is approximately 4.5 billion years old. However, it is only since the late twentieth century, when accurate dating methods were invented and lunar samples obtained by the *Apollo* missions were studied, that the figure became widely accepted. Prior to that time, calculating the age of the Earth was an inexact science resulting in widely differing opinions.

Early attempts to figure out how old the Earth is were based upon geological formations, especially the layering of rocks known as strata. Europe experienced a period of extensive canal building in the 1800s, during which time it was discovered that strata were not always neatly layered horizontally but could be tilted and misshapen in various ways. These discoveries indicated that they had been there a long time and had changed radically as they had aged. Geologists specialized in the study of strata, so they assumed the task of determining the Earth's age. In the eighteenth century, Scottish geologist James Hutton avowed that the Earth's age was without limits as it had neither a beginning nor an end. By the early nineteenth century though, many geologists disagreed with his highly unscientific conclusion that lacked concrete evidence to support it. Nevertheless, calculating the age of the Earth remained problematic for scientists because there was no precise way to utilize strata to discover its age.

*Glossary

radiometric dating: a method of dating objects by analyzing the radioactive material that is in them

strata: layers of material that are piled on top of one another

24 The word "uniform" in the passage is closest in meaning to

(A) reduced

(B) constant

(C) intense

(D) regulated

25 According to paragraph 3, which of the following is NOT true about William Thomson?

(A) He revised his original estimate of the age of the Earth later in his life.

(B) His findings on the age of the Earth were accepted by a large number of geologists.

(C) His research indicated that the Earth is at least twenty million years old.

(D) He tried to determine the Earth's age by figuring out the planet's rate of cooling.

Paragraph 3 is marked with an arrow (➡).

➡ One solution that was proposed suggested that scientists should avoid examining strata but instead look to the laws of thermodynamics. British scientist William Thomson (1824-1907), better known by his title, Lord Kelvin, concluded that the Earth had formed as a molten ball of rock which had a uniform temperature and which had been cooling ever since its creation. He believed that by calculating the rate of cooling to allow the Earth's rocks to solidify, the age of the Earth could be determined. He started with the premise that the Earth was 3,900 degrees Celsius at its formation. Then, Kelvin arrived at the conclusion that the Earth was somewhere between twenty and 400 million years old. The inexactness of his conclusion was the result of the unknown— at that time—exact values of geothermal gradient, which refers to how hot it gets the deeper one descends into the Earth's interior. Kelvin published his findings in 1864 and swiftly became embroiled in a decade-long controversy with geologists. Later, in the 1890s, he caused further debate by estimating that the Earth was only twenty to forty million years old.

26 The author uses "engineer John Perry" as an example of

  (A) the first expert who was able accurately to determine the Earth's age

  (B) a person who did some of the first geological work on the Earth's crust and mantle

  (C) an individual who disagreed with William Thomson regarding the age of the Earth

  (D) one of the people aware of isotopes and how they affected calculations on the Earth's age

27 According to paragraph 5, Ernest Rutherford believed estimates of the Earth's age based upon cooling were incorrect because

  (A) the center of the Earth did not cool off due to the radioactive decay of elements

  (B) scientists could not possibly know how much the Earth had cooled over time

  (C) isotopes in rocks caused geologists to make incorrect guesses about the cooling process

  (D) the rate of radioactive decay in the Earth's center varied due to certain isotopes

Paragraph 5 is marked with an arrow (➡).

28 In paragraph 5, the author implies that *The Age of the Earth*

  (A) was revised several times by Ernest Rutherford

  (B) failed to include an accurate estimate of the age of the Earth

  (C) is considered an authoritative text by geologists today

  (D) contains the results of experiments conducted by leading geologists

Paragraph 5 is marked with an arrow (➡).

The major problem with Kelvin's findings was that he was unaware of another heat source found in the interior of the Earth: radioactivity caused by the decay of isotopes in rocks. As a result of his ignorance, his calculations were widely inaccurate. Kelvin was additionally uninformed of the viscous nature of the planet's interior, especially the mantle, which causes wide fluctuations in the transfer of heat throughout the planet. One of Kelvin's own assistants, engineer John Perry, hypothesized that the Earth consisted of a thin layer of crust resting on top of a fluid mantle. Based upon that theory, in 1895, Perry concluded that the Earth was closer to two or three billion years old. Kelvin, however, refused to accept Perry's calculations and continued to espouse his own conclusions.

➡ The discovery of radiation and methods to measure the radioactive decay of rocks ultimately proved both Kelvin and Perry wrong. In 1904, physicist Ernest Rutherford theorized that radioactive decay in the interior of the Earth kept replenishing the planet's heat supply, so all calculations regarding the age of the Earth based on cooling rates were therefore inaccurate. Eventually, this knowledge of radioactive decay was put to practical use when geologist Arthur Holmes created a method of dating rocks by measuring their rate of radioactive decay in 1911. Two years later in 1913, Holmes published a book entitled *The Age of the Earth*, which called for using radioactive decay as the means to measure the planet's age. Subsequent refinements of his initial work have led scientists to the conclusion that the Earth is in fact roughly 4.5 billion years old.

29 Look at the four squares [■] that indicate where the following sentence could be added to the passage.

He got that number after conducting some experiments during which he melted a variety of rocks.

Where would the sentence best fit?

Click on a square [■] to add the sentence to the passage.

One solution that was proposed suggested that scientists should avoid examining strata but instead look to the laws of thermodynamics. British scientist William Thomson (1824-1907), better known by his title, Lord Kelvin, concluded that the Earth had formed as a molten ball of rock which had a uniform temperature and which had been cooling ever since its creation. He believed that by calculating the rate of cooling to allow the Earth's rocks to solidify, the age of the Earth could be determined. He started with the premise that the Earth was 3,900 degrees Celsius at its formation. **1** Then, Kelvin arrived at the conclusion that the Earth was somewhere between twenty and 400 million years old. **2** The inexactness of his conclusion was the result of the unknown—at that time—exact values of geothermal gradient, which refers to how hot it gets the deeper one descends into the Earth's interior. **3** Kelvin published his findings in 1864 and swiftly became embroiled in a decade-long controversy with geologists. **4** Later, in the 1890s, he caused further debate by estimating that the Earth was only twenty to forty million years old.

30 **Directions:** An introductory sentence for a brief summary of the passage is provided below. Complete the summary by selecting the THREE answer choices that express the most important ideas of the passage. Some sentences do not belong because they express ideas that are not presented in the passage or are minor ideas in the passage. **This question is worth 2 points.**

> Drag your answer choices to the spaces where they belong. To remove an answer choice, click on it. To review the passage, click on **VIEW TEXT**.

During the 1800s and 1900s, scientists estimating the age of the Earth came up with numbers that were widely different from one another.

-
-
-

ANSWER CHOICES

1. John Perry came to the conclusion that the Earth is around twenty to forty million years old.

4. William Thomson's research led him to believe that the Earth is between twenty and 400 million years old.

2. James Hutton did work on the age of the Earth, but it was disregarded as inaccurate by most geologists.

5. Ernest Rutherford believed that using radioactive decay could accurately determine the Earth's age.

3. Lord Kelvin's lack of knowledge of isotopes made him come up with incorrect calculations.

6. A large number of geologists based their estimates on the age of the Earth by studying strata in the ground.

Actual Test

04

Reading Section Directions

This section measures your ability to understand academic passages in English. You will have **54 minutes** to read and answer questions about **3 passages**. A clock at the top of the screen will show you how much time is remaining.

Most questions are worth 1 point but the last question for each passage is worth more than 1 point. The directions for the last question indicate how many points you may receive.

Some passages include a word or phrase that is <u>underlined</u>. Click on the word or phrase to see a definition or an explanation.

When you want to move to the next question, click on **NEXT**. You may skip questions and go back to them later. If you want to return to previous questions, click on **BACK**. You can click on **REVIEW** at any time, and the review screen will show you which questions you have answered and which you have not answered. From this review screen, you may go directly to any question you have already seen in the Reading section.

Click on **CONTINUE** to go on.

The Extinction of the Woolly Mammoth

One of the largest mammals ever to walk the Earth was the mammoth. Comprising around a dozen distinct species, the mammoth was an ancient relative of the modern elephant as it had a similar, but larger, body shape with its long trunk, pair of enormous curved tusks, four huge legs, and tail. The mammoth, however, appeared around five million years ago, so it was much older than the elephant, and, unlike its present-day cousin, it went extinct roughly around 1700 B.C. The exact cause of its extinction is not known, yet scientists have several theories that may explain what happened.

The woolly mammoth was the last species of mammoth to go extinct. It was covered in long brownish fur, which provided protection from the cold in the northern regions of North America, Europe, and Asia, where it resided. For centuries, woolly mammoths were merely legends whose memory was kept alive by generations of people who told tales of great beasts with long tusks and shaggy hair. Then, explorers in the frozen northern tundra began discovering tusks, bones, and even complete frozen mammoth carcasses, the first of which was recovered in Siberia in 1806.

Once the previous existence of the animals was proven, the search for the reason they vanished was initiated. The leading theory was that the conclusion of the ice age roughly 12,000 years ago resulted in a decline in the mammoth's food resources. Examinations of frozen woolly mammoth corpses revealed that they sustained themselves primarily on a diet of various grasses. When the world warmed up, forests began expanding northward, which may have reduced the mammoth's feeding grounds and led to competitions with other animals that the mammoth ultimately lost. There is some evidence that the woolly mammoth suffered a decline in its numbers during a thaw approximately 250,000 years ago; however, the species did not go extinct then and later endured subsequent cycles of thaws and renewed ice ages.

Another theory is that the woolly mammoth was hunted to extinction. After the ice retreated, humans started encroaching upon the lands in which the mammoth resided. A mammoth would have provided a great amount of meat for primitive humans, and, by working together, they would have been able successfully to hunt the great beasts. The first evidence of such hunting comes from a spear point dated to around 15,000 years in the past that paleontologists extracted from the spine of a woolly mammoth. For hundreds of thousands of years, the mammoth had existed across much of northern Eurasia and North America, but, around 14,000 years ago, its range was reduced to a narrow strip along the Eurasian coastline of the Arctic Ocean and a few Arctic islands. While humans definitely hunted them, it is uncertain whether this hunting drove the mammoth to that state, and it is unknown how many mammoths they actually killed.

An additional theory which has some supporters is that disease played a major role in the animal's demise. A new disease the mammoth had no natural protection against could have rapidly wiped

out large numbers of them. Some evidence for this scenario comes from Wrangel Island in the Arctic Ocean. Once connected to the mainland by a land bridge, the island was home to the last population of woolly mammoths. After centuries of being cut off from the mainland by rising seas, the Wrangel Island mammoths evolved to become genetically different and smaller than those in other places. Examinations of the DNA from bones and tusks have proved that this genetic diversity did not cause any weaknesses from the inbreeding that took place among the small population on the island. Nevertheless, when the first humans arrived there around 1600 B.C., the mammoths were gone. Most likely, a sudden catastrophe, such as a plague, killed the remaining Wrangel Island mammoths sometime around 1700 B.C.

Thus far, experts do not agree which of the leading theories played the most significant role in the animal's extinction. In fact, some speculate that all three contributed to the mammoths' deaths. Interestingly, some scientists believe they can reverse the loss by combining DNA found in frozen mammoths with elephant DNA to clone a mammoth-elephant hybrid. With a few generations of crossbreeding, the woolly mammoth might walk the Earth again.

*Glossary

inbreeding: the mating of animals that are closely related to one another

hybrid: the offspring of two animals or plants that are of different species

1 In paragraph 1, the author's description of the mammoth mentions all of the following EXCEPT:

(A) the amount of time that the mammoth existed as a species

(B) the exact reason why the mammoth went extinct

(C) the time when the last mammoth on the Earth died

(D) the number of species of mammoths that there were

Paragraph 1 is marked with an arrow (➡).

2 In paragraph 2, the author implies that the mammoth

(A) was seen by some people who then made up and told stories about it

(B) preferred cold weather but could survive in certain temperate regions

(C) still lived in certain isolated places in Siberia until the nineteenth century

(D) was known to people despite them having no proof that it had existed

Paragraph 2 is marked with an arrow (⇨).

The Extinction of the Woolly Mammoth

➡ One of the largest mammals ever to walk the Earth was the mammoth. Comprising around a dozen distinct species, the mammoth was an ancient relative of the modern elephant as it had a similar, but larger, body shape with its long trunk, pair of enormous curved tusks, four huge legs, and tail. The mammoth, however, appeared around five million years ago, so it was much older than the elephant, and, unlike its present-day cousin, it went extinct roughly around 1700 B.C. The exact cause of its extinction is not known, yet scientists have several theories that may explain what happened.

⇨ The woolly mammoth was the last species of mammoth to go extinct. It was covered in long brownish fur, which provided protection from the cold in the northern regions of North America, Europe, and Asia, where it resided. For centuries, woolly mammoths were merely legends whose memory was kept alive by generations of people who told tales of great beasts with long tusks and shaggy hair. Then, explorers in the frozen northern tundra began discovering tusks, bones, and even complete frozen mammoth carcasses, the first of which was recovered in Siberia in 1806.

More Available ▲

3 The word "sustained" in the passage is closest in meaning to

(A) provided

(B) restored

(C) foraged

(D) supported

4 According to paragraph 3, which of the following is true about the woolly mammoth?

(A) It managed to survive a number of times when the Earth's temperature drastically changed.

(B) It nearly went extinct 250,000 years ago but later increased its numbers considerably.

(C) It was capable of surviving on a reduced diet of vegetation for long periods of time.

(D) It preferred to live on the tundra, but it was also comfortable residing in forested areas.

Paragraph 3 is marked with an arrow (➡).

5 The author uses "a spear point" as an example of

(A) a weapon that was able to kill a woolly mammoth when used properly

(B) evidence that a single spear was not enough for a person to kill a woolly mammoth

(C) a relic that proved humans were in North America more than 15,000 years ago

(D) proof that humans hunted the woolly mammoth thousands of years ago

➡ Once the previous existence of the animals was proven, the search for the reason they vanished was initiated. The leading theory was that the conclusion of the ice age roughly 12,000 years ago resulted in a decline in the mammoth's food resources. Examinations of frozen woolly mammoth corpses revealed that they sustained themselves primarily on a diet of various grasses. When the world warmed up, forests began expanding northward, which may have reduced the mammoth's feeding grounds and led to competitions with other animals that the mammoth ultimately lost. There is some evidence that the woolly mammoth suffered a decline in its numbers during a thaw approximately 250,000 years ago; however, the species did not go extinct then and later endured subsequent cycles of thaws and renewed ice ages.

Another theory is that the woolly mammoth was hunted to extinction. After the ice retreated, humans started encroaching upon the lands in which the mammoth resided. A mammoth would have provided a great amount of meat for primitive humans, and, by working together, they would have been able successfully to hunt the great beasts. The first evidence of such hunting comes from a spear point dated to around 15,000 years in the past that paleontologists extracted from the spine of a woolly mammoth. For hundreds of thousands of years, the mammoth had existed across much of northern Eurasia and North America, but, around 14,000 years ago, its range was reduced to a narrow strip along the Eurasian coastline of the Arctic Ocean and a few Arctic islands. While humans definitely hunted them, it is uncertain whether this hunting drove the mammoth to that state, and it is unknown how many mammoths they actually killed.

6 The word "demise" in the passage is closest in meaning to

(A) downfall

(B) endangerment

(C) descent

(D) weakening

7 According to paragraph 5, the woolly mammoths on Wrangel Island were different than other woolly mammoths because

(A) they suffered various genetic mutations as a result of diseases they caught on the island

(B) the large amount of inbreeding caused them to become larger than other woolly mammoths

(C) they were unable to breed with woolly mammoths that were living on the mainland

(D) the food they ate there was different than that which other woolly mammoths consumed

Paragraph 5 is marked with an arrow (➡).

8 According to paragraph 6, what do some scientists hope to do in the future?

(A) Come to an agreement regarding precisely why the woolly mammoth went extinct

(B) Compare the DNA of the woolly mammoth with that of the modern elephant

(C) Recreate the woolly mammoth by utilizing cloning and crossbreeding with elephants

(D) Make use of cloning to create an elephant that is larger than a woolly mammoth

Paragraph 6 is marked with an arrow (⇨).

➡ An additional theory which has some supporters is that disease played a major role in the animal's demise. A new disease the mammoth had no natural protection against could have rapidly wiped out large numbers of them. Some evidence for this scenario comes from Wrangel Island in the Arctic Ocean. Once connected to the mainland by a land bridge, the island was home to the last population of woolly mammoths. After centuries of being cut off from the mainland by rising seas, the Wrangel Island mammoths evolved to become genetically different and smaller than those in other places. Examinations of the DNA from bones and tusks have proved that this genetic diversity did not cause any weaknesses from the inbreeding that took place among the small population on the island. Nevertheless, when the first humans arrived there around 1600 B.C., the mammoths were gone. Most likely, a sudden catastrophe, such as a plague, killed the remaining Wrangel Island mammoths sometime around 1700 B.C.

⇨ Thus far, experts do not agree which of the leading theories played the most significant role in the animal's extinction. In fact, some speculate that all three contributed to the mammoths' deaths. Interestingly, some scientists believe they can reverse the loss by combining DNA found in frozen mammoths with elephant DNA to clone a mammoth-elephant hybrid. With a few generations of crossbreeding, the woolly mammoth might walk the Earth again.

*Glossary

inbreeding: the mating of animals that are closely related to one another

hybrid: the offspring of two animals or plants that are of different species

More Available ▲

9   Look at the four squares [▪] that indicate where the following sentence could be added to the passage.

Human activity clearly cannot account for their disappearance, so another factor must have been responsible.

Where would the sentence best fit?

Click on a square [▪] to add the sentence to the passage.

An additional theory which has some supporters is that disease played a major role in the animal's demise. A new disease the mammoth had no natural protection against could have rapidly wiped out large numbers of them. Some evidence for this scenario comes from Wrangel Island in the Arctic Ocean. Once connected to the mainland by a land bridge, the island was home to the last population of woolly mammoths. After many centuries of being cut off from the mainland by rising seas, the Wrangel Island woolly mammoths evolved to become genetically different and smaller than those in other places. **1** Examinations of the DNA from bones and tusks have proved that this genetic diversity did not cause any weaknesses from the inbreeding that took place among the small population on the island. **2** Nevertheless, when the first humans arrived there around 1600 B.C., the mammoths were all gone. **3** Most likely, a sudden catastrophe, such as a plague, killed the remaining Wrangel Island woolly mammoths sometime around 1700 B.C. **4**

*Glossary

inbreeding: the mating of animals that are closely related to one another

VIEW TEXT

REVIEW

HELP

BACK

NEXT

HIDE TIME 00:54:00

10 **Directions:** An introductory sentence for a brief summary of the passage is provided below. Complete the summary by selecting the THREE answer choices that express the most important ideas of the passage. Some sentences do not belong because they express ideas that are not presented in the passage or are minor ideas in the passage. **This question is worth 2 points.**

> Drag your answer choices to the spaces where they belong. To remove an answer choice, click on it. To review the passage, click on **VIEW TEXT.**

The woolly mammoth once lived across a wide area of land, but it went extinct around 1700 B.C. for reasons that scientists are not sure of.

-
-
-

ANSWER CHOICES

1 Many woolly mammoths died around 250,000 years ago when the climate changed, but the animal did not go extinct then.

2 There are some scientists who believe that it may be possible to recreate the woolly mammoth by cloning it.

3 Some experts speculate that the last woolly mammoths on Wrangel Island died due to some type of disease.

4 It is possible that hunting by humans resulted in the extinction of the woolly mammoth in certain parts of the world.

5 One of the reasons that the woolly mammoth went extinct may have been due to weather changes when the ice age concluded.

6 The modern-day elephant somewhat resembles the woolly mammoth, but the elephant is larger than the mammoth was.

Free Market and Planned Economies

An economy is a system whereby people exchange money for goods and services. It may operate in a city, region, or country or even on an entire continent. Economies have come to be broadly defined as one of two types: free market and planned economies. Most have elements of both, but, for the most part, one dominates each individual economy. Historically, it has been witnessed repeatedly that free market economies perform much more efficiently than planned economies and therefore provide more benefits to society.

In a free market economy, there is little or no government regulation, so people may do as they wish in the pursuit of profits. In a pure free market economy, people could sell goods and services without any government controls whatsoever. Such an economy does not exist though as there is some degree of government intrusion in every one of the world's economies. For instance, people and businesses must pay taxes, and trade between most nations is regulated to some degree. Governments in turn use the tax revenues they raise to pay for a variety of public services. In addition, by creating rules governing trade, illegal and dangerous products such as narcotics and weapons can be controlled more easily, which makes it hard for smugglers and others to transport, buy, and sell these items.

One of the main advantages of a free market economy is that individuals are extremely motivated to produce high-quality goods and to provide high-quality services. Because their livelihoods depend upon others buying their products or utilizing their services, they realize that if they fail to satisfy their customers, they will be forced into bankruptcy or will go out of business. They are further motivated by the fact that the vast majority of the profits they earn will go into their pockets rather than into the coffers of the government. Resources are also used in an efficient manner in a free market economy because people avoid wasting them out of a desire to earn more money. On the other hand, one of the major disadvantages of a free market economy is that it is subject to instability, which can cause severe inflation, recessions, and depressions and thus result in high prices and unemployment.

Unlike a free market economy, a planned economy involves so much regulation by the government that it determines the majority of aspects of the economy. It has a few benefits though. These include nearly universal employment, stability thanks to regulated prices and wages, the ability to allocate resources where necessary, and a more even distribution of income. Nevertheless, the disadvantages of this type of economy far outweigh its advantages. Centralized government control means that the government needs to collect and utilize vast amounts of information regarding the economy. This requires a large bureaucracy in which individuals wield a great deal of power and which typically leads to corruption at many levels. In addition, a planned economy is inefficient since plans made by bureaucrats frequently ignore economic realities. As for workers, they have little incentive to make good products since their jobs

are not in danger and their wages will remain static no matter how well they work.

Both the Soviet Union and communist China provide two examples of failed planned economies. In the 1920s and 1930s in the Soviet Union, a series of five-year plans were designed to modernize the backward economy of the old tsarist Russia. Goals to bring about this modernization were set yet were unrealistic since they were created by bureaucrats in Moscow who had little understanding of the realities at the mines and in the factories and farming regions. The results were disastrous, especially in the agricultural sector. Soviet plans to forcefully integrate small farmers into large collective farms caused widespread crop failures, especially in the Ukraine, where millions died of starvation in the 1930s. In China, similar disasters resulted from Mao Zedong's planned economic Great Leap Forward in the 1950s. The end result was a massive degradation of the environment and society as a whole. Recognizing the error of its ways, Russia switched to a mostly free market economy after the 1991 collapse of the Soviet Union while China today has a mixed economy of free markets and central planning.

*Glossary

narcotic: a type of substance that can have a soothing or numbing effect on the senses

coffers: a treasury; funds

Free Market and Planned Economies

➡ An economy is a system whereby people exchange money for goods and services. It may operate in a city, region, or country or even on an entire continent. Economies have come to be broadly defined as one of two types: free market and planned economies. Most have elements of both, but, for the most part, one dominates each individual economy. Historically, it has been witnessed repeatedly that free market economies perform much more efficiently than planned economies and therefore provide more benefits to society.

⇨ In a free market economy, there is little or no government regulation, so people may do as they wish in the pursuit of profits. In a pure free market economy, people could sell goods and services without any government controls whatsoever. Such an economy does not exist though as there is some degree of government intrusion in every one of the world's economies. For instance, people and businesses must pay taxes, and trade between most nations is regulated to some degree. Governments in turn use the tax revenues they raise to pay for a variety of public services. In addition, by creating rules governing trade, illegal and dangerous products such as narcotics and weapons can be controlled more easily, which makes it hard for smugglers and others to transport, buy, and sell these items.

11 According to paragraph 1, which of the following is true about free market economies?

  Ⓐ They are practiced more frequently around the world than planned economies are.

  Ⓑ They are better at producing positive results than planned economies are.

  Ⓒ They were only recently introduced to a large number of the world's countries.

  Ⓓ They are efficient when they start but tend to develop problems over time.

Paragraph 1 is marked with an arrow (➡).

12 In paragraph 2, why does the author mention "taxes"?

  Ⓐ To provide an example of how governments get involved in free market economies

  Ⓑ To denounce governments for setting them too high when they should be lower instead

  Ⓒ To point out that they are paid to governments primarily by individuals and companies

  Ⓓ To mention what public works governments use the revenues they raise from taxes on

Paragraph 2 is marked with an arrow (⇨).

13 According to paragraph 2, one benefit of a government getting involved in a free market economy is that

  Ⓐ individuals and businesses are prevented from earning too much money

  Ⓑ trade between two countries can be regulated to a certain extent

  Ⓒ the buying and selling of items that are not legal become harder to do

  Ⓓ smugglers are caught and arrested and therefore cannot operate easily

Paragraph 2 is marked with an arrow (⇨).

*Glossary

narcotic: a type of substance that can have a soothing or numbing effect on the senses

14 According to paragraph 3, individuals are motivated to provide high-quality goods and services in free market economies because

- Ⓐ doing that will enable them to increase the sizes of the companies they own
- Ⓑ they need to do so in order to earn money and to keep from going bankrupt
- Ⓒ they are interested in increasing their reputations with their customers and clients
- Ⓓ it is necessary to pay their taxes to avoid getting in trouble with the government

Paragraph 3 is marked with an arrow (➡).

➡ One of the main advantages of a free market economy is that individuals are extremely motivated to produce high-quality goods and to provide high-quality services. Because their livelihoods depend upon others buying their products or utilizing their services, they realize that if they fail to satisfy their customers, they will be forced into bankruptcy or will go out of business. They are further motivated by the fact that the vast majority of the profits they earn will go into their pockets rather than into the coffers of the government. Resources are also used in an efficient manner in a free market economy because people avoid wasting them out of a desire to earn more money. On the other hand, one of the major disadvantages of a free market economy is that it is subject to instability, which can cause severe inflation, recessions, and depressions and thus result in high prices and unemployment.

*Glossary

coffers: a treasury; funds

More Available

15 The word "allocate" in the passage is closest in meaning to

- Ⓐ seize
- Ⓑ preserve
- Ⓒ distribute
- Ⓓ invest

16 In paragraph 4, the author's description of planned economies mentions all of the following EXCEPT:

- Ⓐ some of the countries in which they have managed to be practiced successfully
- Ⓑ a reason why the bureaucrats operating in them are not very effective
- Ⓒ some ways that they provide advantages for people operating in them
- Ⓓ one of the roles that the government must place in these types of economies

Paragraph 4 is marked with an arrow (➡).

➡ Unlike a free market economy, a planned economy involves so much regulation by the government that it determines the majority of aspects of the economy. It has a few benefits though. These include nearly universal employment, stability thanks to regulated prices and wages, the ability to allocate resources where necessary, and a more even distribution of income. Nevertheless, the disadvantages of this type of economy far outweigh its advantages. Centralized government control means that the government needs to collect and utilize vast amounts of information regarding the economy. This requires a large bureaucracy in which individuals wield a great deal of power and which typically leads to corruption at many levels. In addition, a planned economy is inefficient since plans made by bureaucrats frequently ignore economic realities. As for workers, they have little incentive to make good products since their jobs are not in danger and their wages will remain static no matter how well they work.

17 The word "degradation" in the passage is closest in meaning to

- Ⓐ stagnation
- Ⓑ decline
- Ⓒ oppression
- Ⓓ improvement

18 In paragraph 5, the author implies that tsarist Russia

- Ⓐ had a free market economy until the Soviets replaced it with a planned economy
- Ⓑ relied upon the tsar to determine the manner in which its economy would run
- Ⓒ had an economy that was not considered modern prior to the 1920s
- Ⓓ was stronger economically than either the Soviet Union or communist China

Paragraph 5 is marked with an arrow (➡).

➡ Both the Soviet Union and communist China provide two examples of failed planned economies. In the 1920s and 1930s in the Soviet Union, a series of five-year plans were designed to modernize the backward economy of the old tsarist Russia. Goals to bring about this modernization were set yet were unrealistic since they were created by bureaucrats in Moscow who had little understanding of the realities at the mines and in the factories and farming regions. The results were disastrous, especially in the agricultural sector. Soviet plans to forcefully integrate small farmers into large collective farms caused widespread crop failures, especially in the Ukraine, where millions died of starvation in the 1930s. In China, similar disasters resulted from Mao Zedong's planned economic Great Leap Forward in the 1950s. The end result was a massive degradation of the environment and society as a whole. Recognizing the error of its ways, Russia switched to a mostly free market economy after the 1991 collapse of the Soviet Union while China today has a mixed economy of free markets and central planning.

19 Look at the four squares [■] that indicate where the following sentence could be added to the passage.

Both countries have subsequently seen their economies strengthen and become much better than they were in the past.

Where would the sentence best fit?

Click on a square [■] to add the sentence to the passage.

Both the Soviet Union and communist China provide two examples of failed planned economies. In the 1920s and 1930s in the Soviet Union, a series of five-year plans were designed to modernize the backward economy of the old tsarist Russia. Goals to bring about this modernization were set yet were unrealistic since they were created by bureaucrats in Moscow who had little understanding of the realities at the mines and in the factories and farming regions. The results were disastrous, especially in the agricultural sector. Soviet plans to forcefully integrate small farmers into large collective farms caused widespread crop failures, especially in the Ukraine, where millions died of starvation in the 1930s. **1** In China, similar disasters resulted from Mao Zedong's planned economic Great Leap Forward in the 1950s. **2** The end result was a massive degradation of the environment and society as a whole. **3** Recognizing the error of its ways, Russia switched to a mostly free market economy after the 1991 collapse of the Soviet Union while China today has a mixed economy of free markets and central planning. **4**

20 Directions: Select the appropriate statements from the answer choices and match them to the type of economy to which they relate. TWO of the answer choices will NOT be used. **This question is worth 3 points.**

Drag your answer choices to the spaces where they belong. To remove an answer choice, click on it. To review the passage, click on **VIEW TEXT.**

ANSWER CHOICES

1.   Was the type of economy practiced by the Soviet Union

2.   Involves decisions being made by a small number of powerful individuals

3.   Requires the presence of a large number of people working for the government

4.   Can be unstable at times, which may result in economic crises

5.   Is the type of economy used by most European and Asian countries today

6.   Has as little government involvement in the economy as possible

7.   Is based upon people motivated by the desire to earn money

TYPE OF ECONOMY

Free Market Economy (Select 3)

-
-
-

Planned Economy (Select 2)

-
-

Groundwater

Water trapped beneath the ground yet located near the surface is known as groundwater. An important source of fresh water for human consumption as well as for agricultural purposes, groundwater is additionally a source of replenishment for rivers, lakes, and streams. It serves as the source of fresh water for most living organisms on the Earth, including the majority of plants and animals. However, it is a limited resource since it comprises a mere one percent of all of the Earth's water. Despite being necessary to provide for the needs of people, animals, and plants, groundwater is a vulnerable resource subject to change through both overuse and pollution. As the global human population grows and requires more water and as increased pollution damages sources of groundwater, the amount of clean groundwater available for use declines daily.

Groundwater gathers when it rains or snows and the water seeps into the earth. The water fills the spaces in rocks and soil, particularly in porous rocks such as gravel, sandstone, and limestone, in which water can move easily. Any rock or soil that permits water to flow easily through it is referred to as an aquifer. At some point, the water comes up against rock formations it cannot penetrate, so it gathers in pools. These layers of trapped underground water form the water table. The water table rises and falls depending upon many factors, including human usage, the amount of rainfall, and the amount of snowmelt in a region. Groundwater often ascends to the surface through natural springs or goes up into lakes and rivers. For thousands of years, humans have drilled wells to the water table in order to extract groundwater. Many wells require pumps to help bring the water to the surface, but water that is under pressure and needs no such help is found in artesian wells. Additionally, groundwater often percolates up into the soil and provides water to help plants grow.

Human usage of groundwater varies depending upon the location. People in rural areas lacking substantial rivers or lakes rely heavily on groundwater to sate their personal needs to grow crops. It is estimated that 51% of all Americans use groundwater in some ways and that 99% of rural Americans utilize it. While many big cities are supplied from lakes and reservoirs, these water sources frequently require replenishment from groundwater. Likewise, farms need groundwater as an estimated 64% of American farmers employ it to irrigate their crops. Around the world in rural regions with no manmade water systems, getting groundwater from wells is the only water source for many people.

Unfortunately, overuse and pollution are two major issues concerning groundwater today. The global population stands at seven billion people and is increasing daily, so the demands on groundwater resources are growing. People use it for drinking water and for watering crops to raise more food. As a result, the water table in many regions is at the lowest levels ever recorded. For instance, in parts of India, water table levels are ten meters below normal. The main solution to this problem is to dig deeper wells, but, as they extract more water, the water levels will grow even shallower over time unless there is a substantial increase in the amount of water flowing into the groundwater system. A further problem of overuse is the <u>subsidence</u> of the land above the water table. As water tables grow shallower, the equilibrium between the land surface and the underground mass of land and water becomes unstable. With reduced pressure from less water below, the land on the surface begins sinking, which creates depressions and sometimes even sinkholes.

As for the pollution of groundwater, there are many sources. Localized pollution may come from damaged <u>septic tanks</u> buried on people's property, small petroleum spills, and people burying their garbage in landfills on highly absorbent ground. On a large scale, pollution from farmers using pesticides, miners using chemicals to leech out ores, and factories discharging contaminated water can all cause extensive groundwater pollution. In some cases, groundwater contamination has sickened and even killed people living nearby. Regrettably, not enough is being done to protect groundwater, so there are likely to be problems with both tainted water and shortages in the near future.

*Glossary

subsidence: sinking or falling

septic tank: a tank in which organic sewage is broken down and purified

21 In stating that groundwater is "a vulnerable resource," the author means that groundwater is

- Ⓐ polluted
- Ⓑ at risk
- Ⓒ drinkable
- Ⓓ increasing in amount

22 The author uses "gravel, sandstone, and limestone" as examples of

- Ⓐ three of the most porous rocks that can be found anywhere on the planet
- Ⓑ three kinds of rocks that, when located on the surface, let water seep beneath them
- Ⓒ some of the types of rocks in which it is possible to find groundwater
- Ⓓ rocks that pose few problems for people to drill through while digging wells

23 According to paragraph 2, which of the following is true about the water table?

- Ⓐ It is affected more by rainfall than it is by snowmelt in most regions.
- Ⓑ It has a constant level beneath the surface everywhere on the planet.
- Ⓒ It tends to rise when land is close to a large body of water such as a lake.
- Ⓓ It moves from beneath the ground to the surface in many places.

Paragraph 2 is marked with an arrow (➡).

Groundwater

Water trapped beneath the ground yet located near the surface is known as groundwater. An important source of fresh water for human consumption as well as for agricultural purposes, groundwater is additionally a source of replenishment for rivers, lakes, and streams. It serves as the source of fresh water for most living organisms on the Earth, including the majority of plants and animals. However, it is a limited resource since it comprises a mere one percent of all of the Earth's water. Despite being necessary to provide for the needs of people, animals, and plants, groundwater is a vulnerable resource subject to change through both overuse and pollution. As the global human population grows and requires more water and as increased pollution damages sources of groundwater, the amount of clean groundwater available for use declines daily.

➡ Groundwater gathers when it rains or snows and the water seeps into the earth. The water fills the spaces in rocks and soil, particularly in porous rocks such as gravel, sandstone, and limestone, in which water can move easily. Any rock or soil that permits water to flow easily through it is referred to as an aquifer. At some point, the water comes up against rock formations it cannot penetrate, so it gathers in pools. These layers of trapped underground water form the water table. The water table rises and falls depending upon many factors, including human usage, the amount of rainfall, and the amount of snowmelt in a region. Groundwater often ascends to the surface through natural springs or goes up into lakes and rivers. For thousands of years, humans have drilled wells to the water table in order to extract groundwater. Many wells require pumps to help bring the water to the surface, but water that is under pressure and needs no such help is found in artesian wells. Additionally, groundwater often percolates up into the soil and provides water to help plants grow.

24 The word "sate" in the passage is closest in meaning to

- (A) satisfy
- (B) appoint
- (C) withstand
- (D) consider

25 According to paragraph 3, people in rural areas often depend on groundwater because

- (A) extracting water from the ground in these places is a simple process
- (B) there is a lack of infrastructure for them to get water from other sources
- (C) most rural areas are far from rivers or lakes that can supply them with water
- (D) importing water from other sources is too costly for people in these regions

Paragraph 3 is marked with an arrow (➡).

➡ Human usage of groundwater varies depending upon the location. People in rural areas lacking substantial rivers or lakes rely heavily on groundwater to sate their personal needs to grow crops. It is estimated that 51% of all Americans use groundwater in some ways and that 99% of rural Americans utilize it. While many big cities are supplied from lakes and reservoirs, these water sources frequently require replenishment from groundwater. Likewise, farms need groundwater as an estimated 64% of American farmers employ it to irrigate their crops. Around the world in rural regions with no manmade water systems, getting groundwater from wells is the only water source for many people.

26 Which of the sentences below best expresses the essential information in the highlighted sentence in the passage? Incorrect answer choices change the meaning in important ways or leave out essential information.

The main solution to this problem is to dig deeper wells, but, as they extract more water, the water levels will grow even shallower over time unless there is a substantial increase in the amount of water flowing into the groundwater system.

(A) It is possible to get more water by digging wells that are deeper, but these wells typically go dry once the groundwater in the area is exhausted.

(B) People believe that digging deeper wells can be effective, but it generally merely results in the water level in the surrounding area to decline.

(C) Unless more water is introduced to the groundwater system, then digging deeper wells is not an effective solution to the problem.

(D) When people dig deeper wells, they can get more water, but this depletes water levels more unless the groundwater in the region is replenished.

27 According to paragraph 4, sinkholes may be created when

(A) the amount of water in the ground decreases

(B) more groundwater seeps into porous rock

(C) the water table rises higher than normal

(D) more wells than normal are dug in an area

Paragraph 4 is marked with an arrow (➡).

➡ Unfortunately, overuse and pollution are two major issues concerning groundwater today. The global population stands at seven billion people and is increasing daily, so the demands on groundwater resources are growing. People use it for drinking water and for watering crops to raise more food. As a result, the water table in many regions is at the lowest levels ever recorded. For instance, in parts of India, water table levels are ten meters below normal. The main solution to this problem is to dig deeper wells, but, as they extract more water, the water levels will grow even shallower over time unless there is a substantial increase in the amount of water flowing into the groundwater system. A further problem of overuse is the subsidence of the land above the water table. As water tables grow shallower, the equilibrium between the land surface and the underground mass of land and water becomes unstable. With reduced pressure from less water below, the land on the surface begins sinking, which creates depressions and sometimes even sinkholes.

*Glossary

subsidence: sinking or falling

28 In paragraph 5, the author implies that groundwater

Ⓐ could be kept free of pollution if people made more of an effort to protect it

Ⓑ is likely to disappear entirely in a number of places around the world

Ⓒ has been polluted so much in some places that it is destroying the environment

Ⓓ can be contaminated by salt water from nearby seas and oceans

Paragraph 5 is marked with an arrow (➡).

29 Look at the four squares [■] that indicate where the following sentence could be added to the passage.

It has also caused problems that require many years and huge amounts of money to repair the land and to return it to its original condition.

Where would the sentence best fit?

Click on a square [■] to add the sentence to the passage.

➡ As for the pollution of groundwater, there are many sources. Localized pollution may come from damaged septic tanks buried on people's property, small petroleum spills, and people burying their garbage in landfills on highly absorbent ground. **1** On a large scale, pollution from farmers using pesticides, miners using chemicals to leech out ores, and factories discharging contaminated water can all cause extensive groundwater pollution. **2** In some cases, groundwater contamination has sickened and even killed people living nearby. **3** Regrettably, not enough is being done to protect groundwater, so there are likely to be problems with both tainted water and shortages in the near future. **4**

*Glossary

septic tank: a tank in which organic sewage is broken down and purified

30 **Directions:** An introductory sentence for a brief summary of the passage is provided below. Complete the summary by selecting the THREE answer choices that express the most important ideas of the passage. Some sentences do not belong because they express ideas that are not presented in the passage or are minor ideas in the passage. **This question is worth 2 points.**

Drag your answer choices to the spaces where they belong. To remove an answer choice, click on it. To review the passage, click on **VIEW TEXT**.

Groundwater is an important water source for people around the world, but it is currently suffering from both overuse and pollution.

-
-
-

ANSWER CHOICES

1. There are many factors that cause groundwater to get contaminated, which can then hurt or kill people who drink it.

2. When people use too much groundwater, it can lower the water table and cause the amount of water to diminish.

3. People in both cities and rural areas heavily rely upon groundwater for many of their needs.

4. It is possible for groundwater to be replenished by heavy rains as well as by melting snow in many areas.

5. People frequently dig wells into the ground in order to extract groundwater for various uses.

6. Many countries are making great efforts to prevent their groundwater from becoming too polluted.

106

Actual Test

05

Reading Section Directions

This section measures your ability to understand academic passages in English. You will have **54 minutes** to read and answer questions about **3 passages**. A clock at the top of the screen will show you how much time is remaining.

Most questions are worth 1 point but the last question for each passage is worth more than 1 point. The directions for the last question indicate how many points you may receive.

Some passages include a word or phrase that is <u>underlined</u>. Click on the word or phrase to see a definition or an explanation.

When you want to move to the next question, click on **NEXT**. You may skip questions and go back to them later. If you want to return to previous questions, click on **BACK**. You can click on **REVIEW** at any time, and the review screen will show you which questions you have answered and which you have not answered. From this review screen, you may go directly to any question you have already seen in the Reading section.

Click on **CONTINUE** to go on.

A New Theory on Stonehenge

©Drone Explorer

One of the world's most recognizable ancient structures is Stonehenge, which is comprised of a large number of enormous stones erected upright and positioned in a circular shape. Over the centuries, theories as to why it was built have abounded. The most commonly accepted ones are that people from an ancient culture built it to view the stars, to serve as a burial ground for their dead, or to utilize it as a place of religious significance or healing. Recently, however, a new theory connected to the fact that the builders utilized bluestones as a structural material is gaining some advocates. According to it, bluestones have special acoustic properties that may have permitted ancient Britons to use them to create percussive sounds during rituals held on the site.

Stonehenge was built on the plains of Wiltshire in Western England between 3000 and 1600 B.C. There were various phases of construction, with wood being used in the early periods and stone in the later ones. The massive stones—including the forty-three remaining bluestones—presently there were erected between 2600 and 2500 B.C. Bluestone is the name given to a group of volcanic rocks that have various properties. Dolerite and rhyolite are two kinds of them. The rocks are called bluestones because they give off a bluish color when they are cut or get wet. The bluestones found around Stonehenge are the types containing high levels of feldspar. At one time, it was believed that the largest bluestones, each of which weighs between two and four tons, had been hauled from Pembrokeshire in Wales, a place located approximately 320 kilometers from Stonehenge. Yet the new theory suggests that the bluestones were carried from farther away by glacial action and were then deposited much closer to the current site of Stonehenge.

The facts that a great amount of effort was employed to haul the bluestones to the site from either a long or short distance and that an effort was made to stand them upright mean they must have had some significance to the builders of Stonehenge. Recent archaeological activity on the site by Paul Devereux may have resulted in the discovery of the importance of the stones. Devereux styles himself as an archaeo-acoustic expert, which is a person who uses archaeological methodology to research the manners that ancient cultures utilized sound. Devereux's research team investigated the acoustic properties of thousands of stones in the region of Wales where it is believed that Stonehenge's bluestones came from.

His team discovered that a significant portion of the stones in Wales have strong acoustic properties. In fact, some even sound like bells when struck by smaller stones while others sound like gongs or tin drums. It was also learned that each stone created sounds so different that actual percussive tunes could be played on various rocks that were laid out like a drum kit. In addition, sound reception devices picked up the tones from more than 1.5 kilometers away. After that initial breakthrough, Devereux's team was granted permission to test the bluestones at Stonehenge. To no surprise, it was determined that many of Stonehenge's bluestones could produce various sounds when struck; however, the Stonehenge bluestones had their sound properties somewhat dampened since they had been set upright and placed deep in solid ground.

How the ancient people of Britain used the sound properties remains a mystery though. In modern times, rocks that produce percussion sounds have no particular meaning to individuals, but they may have been significant to people in ancient times. The bluestones at Stonehenge have markings which suggest they had been struck sometime in the past, yet why they were struck is uncertain. Perhaps they were hit during religious ceremonies ancient people carried out. Since bluestones were also thought to have magical healing properties by Britons in the Middle Ages, it is possible that the sound properties of the stones were a secondary factor and that the primary purpose of the stones was to heal sick people coming from various parts of Britain to be cured of whatever was ailing them. It is likely that the original purpose of Stonehenge will never be known with certainty, but individuals will surely keep investigating the area in the hope of discovering it.

*Glossary

percussive: relating to the striking of a musical instrument to produce sound
gong: a large disk that produces a sound when struck by a hammer

1   In paragraph 1, the author's description of
Stonehenge mentions which of the following?

(A) Some possible uses that people had for it
in the past

(B) The number of large stones that it is
comprised of

(C) The real reason that it was constructed in
ancient times

(D) Some of the sounds that can be created
by striking its stones

Paragraph 1 is marked with an arrow (➡).

A New Theory on Stonehenge

➡ One of the world's most recognizable ancient
structures is Stonehenge, which is comprised
of a large number of enormous stones erected
upright and positioned in a circular shape. Over
the centuries, theories as to why it was built have
abounded. The most commonly accepted ones are
that people from an ancient culture built it to view
the stars, to serve as a burial ground for their dead,
or to utilize it as a place of religious significance or
healing. Recently, however, a new theory connected
to the fact that the builders utilized bluestones as
a structural material is gaining some advocates.
According to them, bluestones have special
acoustic properties that may have permitted ancient
Britons to use them to create percussive sounds
during rituals held on the site.

*Glossary

percussive: relating to the striking of a musical instrument to
produce sound

2 What is the author's purpose in paragraph 2?

   Ⓐ To discuss the phases of discussion of Stonehenge in detail

   Ⓑ To describe how the bluestones in Stonehenge were transported there

   Ⓒ To argue that dolerite and rhyolite are the main stones used to make Stonehenge with

   Ⓓ To provide information about the types of stones used to make Stonehenge

Paragraph 2 is marked with an arrow (➡).

3 According to paragraph 2, which of the following is true about the bluestones at Stonehenge?

   Ⓐ There are more than forty different types of them represented at Stonehenge.

   Ⓑ Some of them are believed to have been moved to the Stonehenge area by glaciers.

   Ⓒ Virtually all of them were transported by humans from Pembrokeshire in Wales.

   Ⓓ Several of them have been cut to assess the amount of feldspar that they contain.

Paragraph 2 is marked with an arrow (➡).

➡ Stonehenge was built on the plains of Wiltshire in Western England between 3000 and 1600 B.C. There were various phases of construction, with wood being used in the early periods and stone in the later ones. The massive stones—including the forty-three remaining bluestones—presently there were erected between 2600 and 2500 B.C. Bluestone is the name given to a group of volcanic rocks that have various properties. Dolerite and rhyolite are two kinds of them. The rocks are called bluestones because they give off a bluish color when they are cut or get wet. The bluestones found around Stonehenge are the types containing high levels of feldspar. At one time, it was believed that the largest bluestones, each of which weighs between two and four tons, had been hauled from Pembrokeshire in Wales, a place located approximately 320 kilometers from Stonehenge. Yet the new theory suggests that the bluestones were carried from farther away by glacial action and were then deposited much closer to the current site of Stonehenge.

4 Which of the sentences below best expresses the essential information in the highlighted sentence in the passage? Incorrect answer choices change the meaning in important ways or leave out essential information.

The facts that a great amount of effort was employed to haul the bluestones to the site from either a long or short distance and that an effort was made to stand them upright mean they must have had some significance to the builders of Stonehenge.

(A) It took a great amount of effort for the bluestones first to be taken to Stonehenge and then to be placed in upright positions all over the site.

(B) The creators of Stonehenge must have felt that the bluestones were important since they transported them to the site and then positioned them upright.

(C) There must have been some important reason for all of the bluestones, which weighed a lot, to be carried to Stonehenge and then put into upright positions.

(D) By transporting the bluestones extremely far distances and then putting them in upright positions, the creators of Stonehenge made an important monument.

5 According to paragraph 3, what did Paul Devereux and his team do?

(A) They analyzed the types of sounds the stones of Stonehenge made when struck.

(B) They conducted research on the acoustic properties of various stones in Wales.

(C) They determined which part of Wales the bluestones in Stonehenge came from.

(D) They learned what types of sounds people in ancient cultures were able to make.

Paragraph 3 is marked with an arrow (➡).

➡ The facts that a great amount of effort was employed to haul the bluestones to the site from either a long or short distance and that an effort was made to stand them upright mean they must have had some significance to the builders of Stonehenge. Recent archaeological activity on the site by Paul Devereux may have resulted in the discovery of the importance of the stones. Devereux styles himself as an archaeo-acoustic expert, which is a person who uses archaeological methodology to research the manners that ancient cultures utilized sound. Devereux's research team investigated the acoustic properties of thousands of stones in the region of Wales where it is believed that Stonehenge's bluestones came from.

6 The word "dampened" in the passage is closest in meaning to

(A) soaked

(B) removed

(C) diminished

(D) distorted

7 According to paragraph 4, which of the following is NOT true about Paul Devereux and his team?

(A) They took some of the stones at Stonehenge to their lab to test them for sound properties.

(B) They determined what types of sounds some stones in Wales could make when they are hit.

(C) They learned that many stones at Stonehenge possessed various acoustic properties.

(D) They played music with some of the rocks that they did research on in Wales.

Paragraph 4 is marked with an arrow (➡).

8 In stating that some people went to Stonehenge to be cured of "whatever was ailing them," the author means that these people

(A) suffered from similar problems

(B) were rarely healed

(C) had a variety of illnesses

(D) were cured by the rocks

➡ His team discovered that a significant portion of the stones in Wales have strong acoustic properties. In fact, some even sound like bells when struck by smaller stones while others sound like gongs or tin drums. It was also learned that each stone created sounds so different that actual percussive tunes could be played on various rocks that were laid out like a drum kit. In addition, sound reception devices picked up the tones from more than 1.5 kilometers away. After that initial breakthrough, Devereux's team was granted permission to test the bluestones at Stonehenge. To no surprise, it was determined that many of Stonehenge's bluestones could produce various sounds when struck; however, the Stonehenge bluestones had their sound properties somewhat dampened since they had been set upright and placed deep in solid ground.

How the ancient people of Britain used the sound properties remains a mystery though. In modern times, rocks that produce percussion sounds have no particular meaning to individuals, but they may have been significant to people in ancient times. The bluestones at Stonehenge have markings which suggest they had been struck sometime in the past, yet why they were struck is uncertain. Perhaps they were hit during religious ceremonies ancient people carried out. Since bluestones were also thought to have magical healing properties by Britons in the Middle Ages, it is possible that the sound properties of the stones were a secondary factor and that the primary purpose of the stones was to heal sick people coming from various parts of Britain to be cured of whatever was ailing them. It is likely that the original purpose of Stonehenge will never be known with certainty, but individuals will surely keep investigating the area in the hope of discovering it.

*Glossary

gong: a large disk that produces a sound when struck by a hammer

9   Look at the four squares [■] that indicate where the following sentence could be added to the passage.

Or they may have been struck by people for the purpose of putting on some sort of primitive musical performance.

Where would the sentence best fit?

Click on a square [■] to add the sentence to the passage.

How the ancient people of Britain used the sound properties remains a mystery though. In modern times, rocks that produce percussion sounds have no particular meaning to individuals, but they may have been significant to people in ancient times. The bluestones at Stonehenge have markings which suggest they had been struck sometime in the past, yet why they were struck is uncertain. **1** Perhaps they were hit during religious ceremonies ancient people carried out. **2** Since bluestones were also thought to have magical healing properties by Britons in the Middle Ages, it is possible that the sound properties of the stones were a secondary factor and that the primary purpose of the stones was to heal sick people coming from various parts of Britain to be cured of whatever was ailing them. **3** It is likely that the original purpose of Stonehenge will never be known with certainty, but individuals will surely keep investigating the area in the hope of discovering it. **4**

10 Directions: An introductory sentence for a brief summary of the passage is provided below. Complete the summary by selecting the THREE answer choices that express the most important ideas of the passage. Some sentences do not belong because they express ideas that are not presented in the passage or are minor ideas in the passage. **This question is worth 2 points.**

> Drag your answer choices to the spaces where they belong. To remove an answer choice, click on it. To review the passage, click on **VIEW TEXT**.

There is a new theory about the purpose of Stonehenge that is related to all of the bluestones located at the site.

-
-
-

ANSWER CHOICES

1 There are thousands of rocks in Wales that have been discovered to make unique sounds when they are struck.

2 Paul Devereux and his team have discovered that the bluestones at Stonehenge have acoustic properties.

3 People in the Middle Ages believed that bluestones had healing properties that could make people feel better.

4 It is likely that the bluestones at Stonehenge were considered to be of great importance when they were erected.

5 The sound properties of certain rocks at Stonehenge may have been a reason that large stones were carried there from great distances.

6 Most people are positive that the real reason for the construction of Stonehenge will be discovered one day in the future.

Tecumseh

Tecumseh

Tenskwatawa

In the first few decades after the United States became independent, its greatest enemies were primarily located on the North American continent. One of its fiercest opponents was the Native American chief Tecumseh. The majority of his life was consumed by warfare which resulted from American settlers traveling westward toward the Mississippi River. Becoming the leader of a large confederation of Native American tribes, Tecumseh allied his forces with the British when the War of 1812 broke out between the British and Americans. Although he had many wartime successes, he eventually lost his life in battle.

Tecumseh was born in 1768 and was a member of the Shawnee tribe of Native Americans living in the Ohio region. In 1774, Tecumseh's father was killed in a battle with white settlers attempting to move into the area. Upon reaching manhood, Tecumseh joined his fellow tribe members in trying to prevent more people from settling on Shawnee tribal lands. He led a group that effectively closed traffic on the Ohio River by raiding boats sailing on it. However, after the American War of Independence ended in 1783, American efforts to expand westward intensified. This resulted in the Northwest Indian War of 1789, during which Tecumseh led Shawnee warriors in numerous clashes with American settlers and military forces. The war lasted until 1794, when the Shawnee and their allies were defeated at the Battle of Fallen Timbers. Afterward, virtually the entire Ohio region was <u>ceded</u> to the Americans by the Treaty of Greenville in 1795.

Displeased with the treaty, Tecumseh refused to sign it, yet despite his unhappiness, he kept the peace with white settlers for many years. This peace would not last though. Tecumseh's brother Tenskwatawa became a renowned <u>prophet</u> among the Shawnee by preaching a return to the old ways of life and by urging the Shawnee and other tribes to abandon their acceptance of the American way of life. After a smallpox outbreak devastated many tribes in the Ohio region in 1805, a religious revival among

Native Americans there resulted in many following Tenskwatawa's teachings. This gave Tecumseh a power base to utilize to recommence his conflict with the Americans. Other Shawnee leaders feared renewed warfare, so they forced Tecumseh, Tenskwatawa, and their followers out of Ohio. They moved to nearby Indiana and established the community of Prophetstown.

In 1809, tensions between Tecumseh and the Americans increased after a treaty giving the Americans large tracts of land in Indiana was signed. Tecumseh disapproved of the treaty, and his opposition attracted numerous followers. Then, in 1810, Tecumseh led a large band of warriors to confront the governor of Indiana, William Henry Harrison, at his home. While no blood was spilled there, it set the stage for what became known as Tecumseh's War. In November 1811, Harrison led a thousand soldiers into Shawnee territory and won a victory at the Battle of Tippecanoe. Tecumseh was away recruiting allies, so he missed the fight as his brother led the Native American forces. The lost battle and subsequent burning of Prophetstown dealt a severe blow to the brothers' prestige.

The defeat made Tecumseh more determined to evict the American settlers. He saw an opportunity when the Americans and British went to war in June 1812. Immediately, Tecumseh led 350 warriors into Michigan to unite with British forces marching southward from Canada. In several raids and battles, Tecumseh proved his prowess to the British. When British General Isaac Brock decided to capture the American Fort Detroit, Tecumseh eagerly allied his forces with the general's. On August 15, 1812, they attacked the fort and forced the Americans to surrender. This victory made Tecumseh a great hero both to his people and to the British. They held the fort for a year, but trouble began on September 10, 1813, when an American naval force defeated a British force in the Battle of Lake Erie. This cut off the water supply route through the Great Lakes to Fort Detroit. The British and Native Americans were soon evicted from Fort Detroit and retreated into Canada. On October 5, 1813, they were defeated at the Battle of the Thames. Tecumseh was shot and killed during the fight, which ended the life of a great Native American leader and warrior.

*Glossary

cede: to give something such as land to another person, group, or state

prophet: a person who is believed to be divinely inspired and who speaks for a god or goddess

11 In paragraph 1, the author's description of Tecumseh mentions all of the following EXCEPT:

(A) the manner in which his life came to an end

(B) the reason that he spent many years fighting battles

(C) the side upon which he fought in the War of 1812

(D) the names of some Native American tribes which he led

Paragraph 1 is marked with an arrow (➡).

12 The author discusses "the Northwest Indian War of 1789" in order to

(A) describe in detail the events of the most important battle that was fought during it

(B) portray it as one of the greatest defeats for the Native Americans in the 1700s

(C) emphasize that Tecumseh only had a minor role in the fighting in that war

(D) point out the consequences of certain actions prior to the beginning of the war

13 According to paragraph 2, what did Tecumseh do prior to the American War of Independence?

(A) He trained members of the Shawnee tribe to fight with modern methods.

(B) He led raids of Native Americans against towns founded by white settlers.

(C) He attacked boats that were sailing on the Ohio River in Shawnee territory.

(D) He avenged his father's death by killing a large number of white settlers.

Paragraph 2 is marked with an arrow (⇨).

Tecumseh

➡ In the first few decades after the United States became independent, its greatest enemies were primarily located on the North American continent. One of its fiercest opponents was the Native American chief Tecumseh. The majority of his life was consumed by warfare which resulted from American settlers traveling westward toward the Mississippi River. Becoming the leader of a large confederation of Native American tribes, Tecumseh allied his forces with the British when the War of 1812 broke out between the British and Americans. Although he had many wartime successes, he eventually lost his life in battle.

⇨ Tecumseh was born in 1768 and was a member of the Shawnee tribe of Native Americans living in the Ohio region. In 1774, Tecumseh's father was killed in a battle with white settlers attempting to move into the area. Upon reaching manhood, Tecumseh joined his fellow tribe members in trying to prevent more people from settling on Shawnee tribal lands. He led a group that effectively closed traffic on the Ohio River by raiding boats sailing on it. However, after the American War of Independence ended in 1783, American efforts to expand westward intensified. This resulted in the Northwest Indian War of 1789, during which Tecumseh led Shawnee warriors in numerous clashes with American settlers and military forces. The war lasted until 1794, when the Shawnee and their allies were defeated at the Battle of Fallen Timbers. Afterward, virtually the entire Ohio region was ceded to the Americans by the Treaty of Greenville in 1795.

*Glossary

cede: to give something such as land to another person, group, or state

14 The word "recommence" in the passage is closest in meaning to

- (A) resume
- (B) resort
- (C) repeal
- (D) reveal

15 According to paragraph 3, Tenskwatawa became influential with Native Americans after

- (A) he helped lead the Shawnee to victory in battle against the Americans
- (B) Native Americans expressed a desire to start leading more modern lives
- (C) many Native Americans became interested in religion following a plague
- (D) large numbers of white settlers moved to the region and sickened many Shawnees

Paragraph 3 is marked with an arrow (➡).

16 According to paragraph 4, which of the following is true about Tecumseh's War?

- (A) Tecumseh lost the final battle of the war due to the tactics that he utilized.
- (B) The only battle that was fought during the war was Tecumseh's victory at Tippecanoe.
- (C) The war started when Tecumseh and his army attacked the home of William Henry Harrison.
- (D) It resulted in a defeat in battle for Tecumseh's supporters and the loss of the place they lived.

Paragraph 4 is marked with an arrow (⇨).

➡ Displeased with the treaty, Tecumseh refused to sign it, yet despite his unhappiness, he kept the peace with white settlers for many years. This peace would not last though. Tecumseh's brother Tenskwatawa became a renowned prophet among the Shawnee by preaching a return to the old ways of life and by urging the Shawnee and other tribes to abandon their acceptance of the American way of life. After a smallpox outbreak devastated many tribes in the Ohio region in 1805, a religious revival among Native Americans there resulted in many following Tenskwatawa's teachings. This gave Tecumseh a power base to utilize to recommence his conflict with the Americans. Other Shawnee leaders feared renewed warfare, so they forced Tecumseh, Tenskwatawa, and their followers out of Ohio. They moved to nearby Indiana and established the community of Prophetstown.

⇨ In 1809, tensions between Tecumseh and the Americans increased after a treaty giving the Americans large tracts of land in Indiana was signed. Tecumseh disapproved of land in the treaty, and his opposition attracted numerous followers. Then, in 1810, Tecumseh led a large band of warriors to confront the governor of Indiana, William Henry Harrison, at his home. While no blood was spilled there, it set the stage for what became known as Tecumseh's War. In November 1811, Harrison led a thousand soldiers into Shawnee territory and won a victory at the Battle of Tippecanoe. Tecumseh was away recruiting allies, so he missed the fight as his brother led the Native American forces. The lost battle and subsequent burning of Prophetstown dealt a severe blow to the brothers' prestige.

*Glossary

prophet: a person who is believed to be divinely inspired and who speaks for a god or goddess

End

17 The word "prowess" in the passage is closest in meaning to

- (A) resolve
- (B) honesty
- (C) loyalty
- (D) ability

18 In paragraph 5, the author implies that the Battle of Lake Erie

- (A) was a turning point for British and Native American forces in the War of 1812
- (B) was fought by forces on water as well as by those that were stationed on land
- (C) resulted in the British forces being driven back into the American interior
- (D) was the final battle that was fought by the Americans and British in the War of 1812

Paragraph 5 is marked with an arrow (➡).

➡ The defeat made Tecumseh more determined to evict the American settlers. He saw an opportunity when the Americans and British went to war in June 1812. Immediately, Tecumseh led 350 warriors into Michigan to unite with British forces marching southward from Canada. In several raids and battles, Tecumseh proved his prowess to the British. When British General Isaac Brock decided to capture the American Fort Detroit, Tecumseh eagerly allied his forces with the general's. On August 15, 1812, they attacked the fort and forced the Americans to surrender. This victory made Tecumseh a great hero both to his people and to the British. They held the fort for a year, but trouble began on September 10, 1813, when an American naval force defeated a British force in the Battle of Lake Erie. This cut off the water supply route through the Great Lakes to Fort Detroit. The British and Native Americans were soon evicted from Fort Detroit and retreated into Canada. On October 5, 1813, they were defeated at the Battle of the Thames. Tecumseh was shot and killed during the fight, which ended the life of a great Native American leader and warrior.

19 Look at the four squares [■] that indicate where the following sentence could be added to the passage.

He would later use this triumph as a part of a slogan to promote himself while successfully running for president of the United States in 1840.

Where would the sentence best fit?

Click on a square [■] to add the sentence to the passage.

In 1809, tensions between Tecumseh and the Americans increased after a treaty giving the Americans large tracts of land in Indiana was signed. Tecumseh disapproved of the treaty, and his opposition attracted numerous followers. Then, in 1810, Tecumseh led a large band of warriors to confront the governor of Indiana, William Henry Harrison, at his home. **1** While no blood was spilled there, it set the stage for what became known as Tecumseh's War. **2** In November 1811, Harrison led a thousand soldiers into Shawnee territory and won a victory at the Battle of Tippecanoe. **3** Tecumseh was away recruiting allies, so he missed the fight as his brother led the Native American forces. **4** The lost battle and subsequent burning of Prophetstown dealt a severe blow to the brothers' prestige.

20 Directions: An introductory sentence for a brief summary of the passage is provided below. Complete the summary by selecting the THREE answer choices that express the most important ideas of the passage. Some sentences do not belong because they express ideas that are not presented in the passage or are minor ideas in the passage. **This question is worth 2 points.**

Drag your answer choices to the spaces where they belong. To remove an answer choice, click on it. To review the passage, click on **VIEW TEXT**.

The Native American Tecumseh was a great enemy of the United States who fought many battles against the Americans.

-
-
-

ANSWER CHOICES

1. Tecumseh and his brother Tenskwatawa led many Native Americans, but they were defeated in battle during Tecumseh's War.

2. There was a time that lasted many years during which Tecumseh took no offensive action against American settlers.

3. Shawnee warriors led by Tecumseh fought alongside the British in several battles during the War of 1812.

4. Tecumseh and his men were unable to contribute to the fighting during the Battle of Lake Erie in the War of 1812.

5. Tecumseh's father was killed in a fight with white settlers when Tecumseh was a child, and that made him hate Americans.

6. Tecumseh and his warriors engaged in a large number of fights against white settlers in the 1770s and 1780s.

Parasitism

a dodder plant parasite

Parasites, which are organisms that live off other ones, often afflict organisms in both the plant and animal kingdoms. While parasites usually require a host—the plant or animal they live off of—in order to survive, they come in a wide variety of forms. The actions of parasites harm their hosts in some manner, yet parasites almost never intentionally kill them since they are necessary for parasites to survive. Parasites are most commonly bacteria, viruses, and fungi, yet they can be insects, protozoa, and worms as well, and there are even around 4,000 species of plants considered parasites.

Parasites can be divided into obligate parasites, which need at least one host and sometimes two or more to complete their life cycles, and facultative parasites, which do not require a host for that. An example of an obligate parasite is the bilharzias parasite, which is a type of flatworm that uses humans and snails to complete its life cycle. An adult male and female live in a human's blood vessels, where they mate. When the female is ready to lay her eggs, she moves to the person's bladder. After the eggs are laid, they are released from the body through urination, whereupon they come into contact with water. This enables the eggshells to break, so the larvae are released. Each larva must find a snail, enter its body, and then begin growing. Later, the bilharzias must depart the snail's body, reenter water, and find its way into a human body to reach maturity, mate, and complete its life cycle. Facultative parasites, on the other hand, require no host to complete their life cycles. Many species of fungi that attack plants are these kinds of parasites. The plants they infest serve merely as sources of nutrition and are not means for the parasite to reproduce or to complete its life cycle.

It is also possible to describe parasites according to whether they live outside or inside their hosts' bodies. Parasites residing on the surfaces of their hosts' bodies are ectoparasites. Among them are ticks, mites, and lice, including head lice, which make their homes in human hair. Parasites that live inside their hosts' bodies are known as endoparasites and include many species of bacteria, protozoa, and viruses. Endoparasites can be further subdivided into those living in spaces in their hosts' bodies and those directly invading the cells of their hosts. A third type of parasite is the epiparasite, which lives inside another parasite that itself lives off a host. An example of it is a virus or bacterium residing inside a tick or flea which is living off an animal host.

There are a variety of ways for parasites to invade their hosts. Most animal parasites accomplish that by directly burrowing into the skin or by lying on the skin or in the hair. Others may also live in water or food until their hosts ingest it. Most plant parasites, however, directly attack plants. In general, the seeds of a plant parasite must be lying close to the host before they will germinate. Chemical signals indicate to the seeds that a host plant is nearby, so the seeds germinate, grow, and attach themselves to the host plant. Following those actions, the parasite plant utilizes its root system to secure itself to the host. The dodder plant parasite acts in this manner by infesting non-woody plants such as clover, grass, and wheat and absorbing its host's nutrients and water. Once dodder gets established in an area of dense plant growth, it spreads rapidly to other nearby plants.

Hosts are not completely defenseless when attacked by parasites but actually have a number of ways to shield themselves. In humans and animals, the skin is the first line of defense against endoparasites, and saliva, along with internal digestive tract acids, can destroy many types of parasites as can human and animal immune systems. Humans have additionally devised other ways to eradicate parasites. For instance, there are medicines that can kill specific parasites, and other parasite-killing products, such as special shampoos, can eliminate head lice infestations. As for plants, many are capable of producing chemicals that can prevent parasites from spreading any further.

*Glossary

larva: an immature insect that is in its feeding stage
eradicate: to destroy completely; to wipe out

21 In paragraph 1, the author's description of parasites mentions which of the following?

- Ⓐ The approximate number of parasites that exist in the world
- Ⓑ The types of organisms that are often preyed upon by parasites
- Ⓒ The sizes of most parasites in comparison with their hosts'
- Ⓓ The reason that many parasites wind up being fatal to their hosts

Paragraph 1 is marked with an arrow (➡).

22 In paragraph 2, the author's description of the bilharzias parasite mentions all of the following EXCEPT:

- Ⓐ which kind of parasite it is considered to be because of how it acts
- Ⓑ the manner in which its eggs depart from the body that they are in
- Ⓒ which animals are necessary in order for it to complete its life cycle
- Ⓓ the type of harm that it can do to the host whose body it is in

Paragraph 2 is marked with an arrow (⇨).

Parasitism

➡ Parasites, which are organisms that live off other ones, often afflict organisms in both the plant and animal kingdoms. While parasites usually require a host—the plant or animal they live off of—in order to survive, they come in a wide variety of forms. The actions of parasites harm their hosts in some manner, yet parasites almost never intentionally kill them since they are necessary for parasites to survive. Parasites are most commonly bacteria, viruses, and fungi, yet they can be insects, protozoa, and worms as well, and there are even around 4,000 species of plants considered parasites.

⇨ Parasites can be divided into obligate parasites, which need at least one host and sometimes two or more to complete their life cycles, and facultative parasites, which do not require a host for that. An example of an obligate parasite is the bilharzias parasite, which is a type of flatworm that uses humans and snails to complete its life cycle. An adult male and female live in a human's blood vessels, where they mate. When the female is ready to lay her eggs, she moves to the person's bladder. After the eggs are laid, they are released from the body through urination, whereupon they come into contact with water. This enables the eggshells to break, so the larvae are released. Each larva must find a snail, enter its body, and then begin growing. Later, the bilharzias must depart the snail's body, reenter water, and find its way into a human body to reach maturity, mate, and complete its life cycle. Facultative parasites, on the other hand, require no host to complete their life cycles. Many species of fungi that attack plants are these kinds of parasites. The plants they infest serve merely as sources of nutrition and are not means for the parasite to reproduce or to complete its life cycle.

*Glossary

larva: an immature insect that is in its feeding stage

23 The author uses "ticks, mites, and lice" as examples of

- Ⓐ parasites that only live in human hair
- Ⓑ parasites that live on the bodies of their hosts
- Ⓒ parasites that are known to sicken their hosts
- Ⓓ parasites that live inside the bodies of their hosts

24 According to paragraph 3, the epiparasite differs from other parasites because

- Ⓐ it causes no actual harm to any of the hosts whose bodies it lives in
- Ⓑ it resides in the body of a parasite that is living off another organism
- Ⓒ it spends its entire life cycle living inside the body of its host
- Ⓓ it resides in the bodies of two or more different types of hosts

Paragraph 3 is marked with an arrow (➡).

25 The word "ingest" in the passage is closest in meaning to

- Ⓐ prepare
- Ⓑ consume
- Ⓒ digest
- Ⓓ regurgitate

26 According to paragraph 4, the dodder plant gets nourishment by

- Ⓐ extracting nutrients from the body of an animal
- Ⓑ using chemicals that are found in its body
- Ⓒ absorbing it from the ground and the air
- Ⓓ taking it from the host in which it lives

Paragraph 4 is marked with an arrow (⇨).

➡ It is also possible to describe parasites according to whether they live outside or inside their hosts' bodies. Parasites residing on the surfaces of their hosts' bodies are ectoparasites. Among them are ticks, mites, and lice, including head lice, which make their homes in human hair. Parasites that live inside their hosts' bodies are known as endoparasites and include many species of bacteria, protozoa, and viruses. Endoparasites can be further subdivided into those living in spaces in their hosts' bodies and those directly invading the cells of their hosts. A third type of parasite is the epiparasite, which lives inside another parasite that itself lives off a host. An example of it is a virus or bacterium residing inside a tick or flea which is living off an animal host.

⇨ There are a variety of ways for parasites to invade their hosts. Most animal parasites accomplish that by directly burrowing into the skin or by lying on the skin or in the hair. Others may also live in water or food until their hosts ingest it. Most plant parasites, however, directly attack plants. In general, the seeds of a plant parasite must be lying close to the host before they will germinate. Chemical signals indicate to the seeds that a host plant is nearby, so the seeds germinate, grow, and attach themselves to the host plant. Following those actions, the parasite plant utilizes its root system to secure itself to the host. The dodder plant parasite acts in this manner by infesting non-woody plants such as clover, grass, and wheat and absorbing its host's nutrients and water. Once dodder gets established in an area of dense plant growth, it spreads rapidly to other nearby plants.

End ▲

27 The word "shield" in the passage is closest in meaning to

(A) disinfect

(B) strengthen

(C) protect

(D) empower

28 In paragraph 5, the author implies that parasites

(A) may be in some danger of going extinct due to advances in medicine

(B) are considered harmful by humans, who seek ways to destroy them

(C) continually evolve to defeat efforts by other organisms to kill them

(D) can be defeated by various vaccinations that human scientists create

Paragraph 5 is marked with an arrow (➡).

➡ Hosts are not completely defenseless when attacked by parasites but actually have a number of ways to shield themselves. In humans and animals, the skin is the first line of defense against endoparasites, and saliva, along with internal digestive tract acids, can destroy many types of parasites as can human and animal immune systems. Humans have additionally devised other ways to eradicate parasites. For instance, there are medicines that can kill specific parasites, and other parasite-killing products, such as special shampoos, can eliminate head lice infestations. As for plants, many are capable of producing chemicals that can prevent parasites from spreading any further.

*Glossary

eradicate: to destroy completely; to wipe out

29 Look at the four squares [■] that indicate where the following sentence could be added to the passage.

Other parasites that behave in a manner similar to bilharzias are the plasmodium protozoans that cause malaria and the bacteria Coxiella burnetii, which cause Q fever.

Where would the sentence best fit?

Click on a square [■] to add the sentence to the passage.

Parasites can be divided into obligate parasites, which need at least one host and sometimes two or more to complete their life cycles, and facultative parasites, which do not require a host for that. An example of an obligate parasite is the bilharzias parasite, which is a type of flatworm that uses humans and snails to complete its life cycle. An adult male and female live in a human's blood vessels, where they mate. When the female is ready to lay her eggs, she moves to the person's bladder. After the eggs are laid, they are released from the body through urination, whereupon they come into contact with water. This enables the eggshells to break, so the larvae are released. Each larva must find a snail, enter its body, and then begin growing. Later, the bilharzias must depart the snail's body, reenter water, and find its way into a human body to reach maturity, mate, and complete its life cycle. **1** Facultative parasites, on the other hand, require no host to complete their life cycles. **2** Many species of fungi that attack plants are these kinds of parasites. **3** The plants they infest serve merely as sources of nutrition and are not means for the parasite to reproduce or to complete its life cycle. **4**

*Glossary

larva: an immature insect that is in its feeding stage

30 Directions: An introductory sentence for a brief summary of the passage is provided below. Complete the summary by selecting the THREE answer choices that express the most important ideas of the passage. Some sentences do not belong because they express ideas that are not presented in the passage or are minor ideas in the passage. **This question is worth 2 points.**

Drag your answer choices to the spaces where they belong. To remove an answer choice, click on it. To review the passage, click on **VIEW TEXT**.

There are many different types of parasites, all of which live off their hosts and generally cause harm to them in some manner.

-
-
-

ANSWER CHOICES

1. There are some medicines that can fight parasites and enable them to be removed from people's bodies.

2. Plant and animal parasites can attack their hosts in many ways, but hosts are also capable of defending themselves.

3. While obligate parasites require one or more hosts in order to live, facultative parasites do not require a host to survive.

4. Bacteria, fungi, and viruses are the most common types of parasites, but plants, worms, insects, and protozoa can also be parasites.

5. The dodder plant is a parasite that lives in plants such as wheat and clover and which can spread at a very swift rate.

6. The host of a parasite is most commonly a plant or an animal, and it can have a variety of reactions to the parasite.

Actual Test

06

Reading Section Directions

This section measures your ability to understand academic passages in English. You will have **54 minutes** to read and answer questions about **3 passages**. A clock at the top of the screen will show you how much time is remaining.

Most questions are worth 1 point but the last question for each passage is worth more than 1 point. The directions for the last question indicate how many points you may receive.

Some passages include a word or phrase that is <u>underlined</u>. Click on the word or phrase to see a definition or an explanation.

When you want to move to the next question, click on **NEXT**. You may skip questions and go back to them later. If you want to return to previous questions, click on **BACK**. You can click on **REVIEW** at any time, and the review screen will show you which questions you have answered and which you have not answered. From this review screen, you may go directly to any question you have already seen in the Reading section.

Click on **CONTINUE** to go on.

The Trivium and the Quadrivium in Medieval Education

While the Middle Ages are often referred to as the Dark Ages in the implication that little learning occurred during that period, there was actually a great amount of education happening during medieval times. In fact, European educators at universities in the Middle Ages devised a curriculum of seven liberal arts that were based on the teaching methods of ancient Greece and were outlined by Plato in his seminal work *The Republic*. These liberal arts were arranged in two sets of skills and knowledge and were known as the trivium and the quadrivium.

The objective of the seven liberal arts was to train the mind to think rather than being told what to think. By observing the world with the five senses—sight, hearing, taste, touch, and smell—a person acquired knowledge. How the person interpreted it depended upon how his mind was trained to think. By using the methods learned in the study of the trivium and the quadrivium, a person could understand new things based upon what he already knew. The person could then explain new things to others and would know how to store this new information in his mind.

The trivium consisted of three skills: grammar, logic, and rhetoric. As for the quadrivium, it was comprised of the skills known as arithmetic, geometry, music, and astronomy. The trivium was the equivalent of a modern-day bachelor of arts while the quadrivium was a more advanced field of study akin to a master's degree. The skills students learned by studying the trivium prepared them for the higher level of learning entailed in the study of the quadrivium. Upon completing all seven subjects, a student's basic formal education was complete. Those who wished to pursue further studies engaged in the academic disciplines of philosophy, medicine, law, or theology.

The most basic course of study in the trivium was grammar, which had to be mastered to permit the understanding of language and the written word. Spoken language and writing were the primary methods used to understand the world and to learn knowledge. The teaching of grammar was subdivided into four areas: prose, meter, rhythm, and poetry. By studying those four topics, medieval students learned to create meaning from words and to order their thoughts to express them with words when speaking and writing. Once a student mastered it, he moved to the more difficult concepts of logic and rhetoric. Logic, often called dialectic, was a form of reasoning wherein dialogue and debate were utilized to reach conclusions on various topics. It was frequently used by medieval scholars to find the truths of many subjects, especially religious questions. Rhetoric, the last subject in the trivium, focused on presenting ideas in formal writing and speeches. Students had to learn a set way to present information, particularly with respect to arranging and delivering it when speaking and writing.

All four subjects in the quadrivium were based on numbers. The main thematic concept of the quadrivium was the study of numbers and their relation to space and time. Arithmetic focused on numbers by themselves in pure abstraction with no relation to space or time while geometry stressed numbers as related to space. As for music, it focused on numbers in time whereas astronomy was about how numbers related to both time and space.

During the Middle Ages, the study of those four subjects was unlike how they are presently studied. Arithmetic mainly involved the study of theories related to numbers and was based on the teachings of the Greek Aristotle regarding the relationships between numbers, especially ratios. The study of astronomy centered on Plato's teachings that the universe consisted of ten spheres and focused on their relationships as they rotated around one another. Geometry was concerned with measurements and ratios, including how God was related to everything he created. Music was studied not to learn to play or compose it but to understand its nature because it was believed to be a method of expressing numbers through sound. As such, music was thought to be an expression of ratios.

It frequently took several years for medieval students to complete their studies of the trivium and the quadrivium. Those who did so were considered among the most educated individuals during that period of time.

*Glossary

medieval: relating to the Middle Ages

ratio: a proportional relation between two numbers

The Trivium and the Quadrivium in Medieval Education

➡ While the Middle Ages are often referred to as the Dark Ages in the implication that little learning occurred during that period, there was actually a great amount of education happening during medieval times. In fact, European educators at universities in the Middle Ages devised a curriculum of seven liberal arts that were based on the teaching methods of ancient Greece and were outlined by Plato in his seminal work *The Republic*. These liberal arts were arranged in two sets of skills and knowledge and were known as the trivium and the quadrivium.

⇨ The objective of the seven liberal arts was to train the mind to think rather than being told what to think. By observing the world with the five senses—sight, hearing, taste, touch, and smell—a person acquired knowledge. How the person interpreted it depended upon how his mind was trained to think. By using the methods learned in the study of the trivium and the quadrivium, a person could understand new things based upon what he already knew. The person could then explain new things to others and would know how to store this new information in his mind.

1 The word "seminal" in the passage is closest in meaning to

Ⓐ popular

Ⓑ influential

Ⓒ biographical

Ⓓ fictional

2 According to paragraph 1, which of the following is true about education in the Middle Ages?

Ⓐ It is generally regarded as being inferior to what was taught in ancient Greece.

Ⓑ It was based solely on the ancient Greek work *The Republic*, which was written by Plato.

Ⓒ It was heavily influenced by learning from ancient Greece, including that of Plato.

Ⓓ It involved the training of young men in Greek history when they attended universities.

Paragraph 1 is marked with an arrow (➡).

3 According to paragraph 2, people studied the trivium and the quadrivium in order to

Ⓐ become more knowledgeable by relying on their senses to acquire information

Ⓑ learn how to focus their senses so that they could rely on them instead of their minds

Ⓒ get as much information as they could and then learn how they could teach others

Ⓓ be told what to think by their instructors so that they could pass on the information later

Paragraph 2 is marked with an arrow (⇨).

*Glossary

medieval: relating to the Middle Ages

4 In paragraph 3, which of the following can be inferred about the trivium and the quadrivium?

(A) Students needed to learn both Greek and Latin in order to complete their studies of them.

(B) The order in which they were studied was not considered to be of great importance.

(C) They were not only taught to university students but were also taught to younger students.

(D) A person had to master both of them before he could study law at a medieval university.

Paragraph 3 is marked with an arrow (➡).

5 According to paragraph 4, how did people in the Middle Ages use logic?

(A) To organize the way in which they thought about topics

(B) To learn the truth about various questions of a religious nature

(C) To make speeches to convince others of the correctness of their opinions

(D) To learn more about both prose and poetry

Paragraph 4 is marked with an arrow (⇨).

➡ The trivium consisted of three skills: grammar, logic, and rhetoric. As for the quadrivium, it was comprised of the skills known as arithmetic, geometry, music, and astronomy. The trivium was the equivalent of a modern-day bachelor of arts while the quadrivium was a more advanced field of study akin to a master's degree. The skills students learned by studying the trivium prepared them for the higher level of learning entailed in the study of the quadrivium. Upon completing all seven subjects, a student's basic formal education was complete. Those who wished to pursue further studies engaged in the academic disciplines of philosophy, medicine, law, or theology.

⇨ The most basic course of study in the trivium was grammar, which had to be mastered to permit the understanding of language and the written word. Spoken language and writing were the primary methods used to understand the world and to learn knowledge. The teaching of grammar was subdivided into four areas: prose, meter, rhythm, and poetry. By studying those four topics, medieval students learned to create meaning from words and to order their thoughts to express them with words when speaking and writing. Once a student mastered it, he moved to the more difficult concepts of logic and rhetoric. Logic, often called dialectic, was a form of reasoning wherein dialogue and debate were utilized to reach conclusions on various topics. It was frequently used by medieval scholars to find the truths of many subjects, especially religious questions. Rhetoric, the last subject in the trivium, focused on presenting ideas in formal writing and speeches. Students had to learn a set way to present information, particularly with respect to arranging and delivering it when speaking and writing.

6 The word "stressed" in the passage is closest in meaning to

   Ⓐ researched

   Ⓑ calculated

   Ⓒ emphasized

   Ⓓ approached

7 According to paragraph 5, which of the following is NOT true about the quadrivium?

   Ⓐ The study of abstract numbers was done in arithmetic.

   Ⓑ Numbers in relation to both space and time were learned in astronomy.

   Ⓒ Numbers were the primary focus of all the subjects in it.

   Ⓓ The study of music avoided the learning of numbers.

Paragraph 5 is marked with an arrow (➡).

8 In paragraph 6, why does the author mention "the Greek Aristotle"?

   Ⓐ To provide a brief summary of his contributions to the field of education

   Ⓑ To compare the quality of his work with that of the Greek Plato

   Ⓒ To claim that people in the Middle Ages considered him the greatest philosopher

   Ⓓ To state that a part of the quadrivium was based on the work he produced

Paragraph 6 is marked with an arrow (⇨).

➡ All four subjects in the quadrivium were based on numbers. The main thematic concept of the quadrivium was the study of numbers and their relation to space and time. Arithmetic focused on numbers by themselves in pure abstraction with no relation to space or time while geometry stressed numbers as related to space. As for music, it focused on numbers in time whereas astronomy was about how numbers related to both time and space.

⇨ During the Middle Ages, the study of those four subjects was unlike how they are presently studied. Arithmetic mainly involved the study of theories related to numbers and was based on the teachings of the Greek Aristotle regarding the relationships between numbers, especially ratios. The study of astronomy centered on Plato's teachings that the universe consisted of ten spheres and focused on their relationships as they rotated around one another. Geometry was concerned with measurements and ratios, including how God was related to everything he created. Music was studied not to learn to play or compose it but to understand its nature because it was believed to be a method of expressing numbers through sound. As such, music was thought to be an expression of ratios.

It frequently took several years for medieval students to complete their studies of the trivium and quadrivium. Those who did so were considered among the most educated individuals during that period of time.

*Glossary

ratio: a proportional relation between two numbers

More Available ▲

9   Look at the four squares [■] that indicate where the following sentence could be added to the passage.

Thus more students completed their studies of the trivium than those who went on to master the quadrivium as well.

Where would the sentence best fit?

Click on a square [■] to add the sentence to the passage.

■ The trivium consisted of three skills: grammar, logic, and rhetoric. ■ As for the quadrivium, it was comprised of the skills known as arithmetic, geometry, music, and astronomy. ■ The trivium was the equivalent of a modern-day bachelor of arts while the quadrivium was a more advanced field of study akin to a master's degree. ■ The skills students learned by studying the trivium prepared them for the higher level of learning entailed in the study of the quadrivium. Upon completing all seven subjects, a student's basic formal education was complete. Those who wished to pursue further studies engaged in the academic disciplines of philosophy, medicine, law, or theology.

▼

10 **Directions:** Select the appropriate statements from the answer choices and match them to the liberal art to which they relate. TWO of the answer choices will NOT be used. **This question is worth 3 points.**

Drag your answer choices to the spaces where they belong. To remove an answer choice, click on it. To review the passage, click on **VIEW TEXT**.

ANSWER CHOICES

1. Taught the proper way to organize information

2. Was the major field of study for theology students

3. Emphasized the study of ancient Greek and classical Latin

4. Involved the study of measurements and ratios

5. Allowed students to put their thoughts into words

6. Explored the relationships of the ten spheres in the universe

7. Focused on the study of meter and rhythm

LIBERAL ART

Trivium (Select 3)

-
-
-

Quadrivium (Select 2)

-
-

The East Asian-Australasian Flyway

Every year, numerous species of migratory birds fly south for the winter and then return northward when warmer weather arrives. Billions of birds follow flyways, which are corridors popular with various species and which enable them to visit their breeding grounds and to avoid the extreme temperatures occurring in polar and temperate regions. There are eight major flyways located around the world. One of the longest is the East Asian-Australasian Flyway, which stretches from northern Russia and Alaska into eastern Asia and goes south to Australia and New Zealand.

The East Asian-Australasian Flyway covers a territory encompassing roughly eighty-five million square kilometers of land and water. There are thirty-seven countries, including the United States, Russia, China, Korea, Japan, India, the Philippines, Indonesia, Australia, and New Zealand, that birds migrate through by using it. Zoologists have thus far identified 492 distinct species of migratory birds that use the flyway and estimate that up to fifty million birds traverse it every year. Most are water birds, including up to eight million of which are birds that ornithologists call waders. These birds primarily reside in shallow water and depend upon marine life forms for sustenance.

How the birds move along the East Asian-Australasian Flyway depends upon the individual species. Most move in stages by making short flights from one place to another. They often use the same staging areas year after year, so preserving these areas is crucial for the survival of some species. For instance, the lesser sand plover uses the Yellow Sea route through parts of Korea and China and stops at the same places on each stage of its journey. Another species, the whimbrel, annually flies along the same rivers in Russia as it moves north and south. The species with the longest migration on the flyway is the bar-tailed godwit, which flies almost 11,000 kilometers over the Pacific Ocean from its breeding grounds in Alaska all the way down to New Zealand. When it flies back north, it takes a different route as it flies above the Western Pacific Ocean, crosses Korea and Japan, and then moves up the Aleutian Island chain to return to Alaska.

Among the birds that use the flyway, sixty-four species are considered endangered, and seven are critical, meaning they are nearly extinct. These species—and others—face numerous threats while they migrate. One of the biggest dangers is human hunting. While international agreements that protect the birds and their breeding grounds are making some headway, they do not cover every site. Of the approximately 1,100 sites the birds use in their travels, more than 600 are protected. Of the remainder, 272 are partially protected while the others are unprotected. Another major threat to the birds is the stresses that occur on account of them making such long journeys. These include attacks from predators, the need to acquire food, and the dangers posed by unfavorable weather conditions. Additionally, diseases, particularly avian botulism and avian influenza, take a toll on the birds each year. In 2002 and 2003, a

botulism outbreak in Taiwan killed seven percent of the world's black-faced spoonbill population while an outbreak of influenza in China in 2005 decimated an estimated ten percent of the bar-headed geese population.

While those issues all pose problems for the birds, the greatest peril they face is that humans will develop their staging areas and breeding grounds. Of all the flyways, the East Asian-Australasian Flyway has the greatest human population, and, as such, the land beneath it is constantly being developed. In China, thirty-seven percent of its intertidal waterways have been lost to land reclamation projects in recent decades. In South Korea, the figure stands at forty-three percent. The spoon-billed sandpiper, which migrates from Russia to Southeast Asia by way of China each year, has lost most of its staging areas since the 1970s. As a result, by 2005, zoologists only counted 350 breeding pairs, which made it a nearly extinct species.

Unfortunately, efforts to stop land reclamation projects have been stymied by the growing pressures of exploding populations and the desires of people to use more land for housing and other projects. In the end, unless people take steps to protect more staging areas, large parts of the East Asian-Australasian Flyway may become empty skies.

*Glossary

ornithologist: a person who studies birds

intertidal: relating to the water around a shore that is above the low-water mark and beneath the high-water mark

Beginning ▲

11 The word "corridors" in the passage is closest in meaning to

　Ⓐ hallways

　Ⓑ currents

　Ⓒ passages

　Ⓓ roads

12 In paragraph 1, the author's description of the East Asian-Australasian Flyway mentions all of the following EXCEPT:

　Ⓐ the countries in which it begins and ends

　Ⓑ which types of animals make use of it

　Ⓒ the months during which it is at its busiest

　Ⓓ how large it is in relation to other flyways

Paragraph 1 is marked with an arrow (➡).

13 According to paragraph 2, which of the following is true about the East Asian-Australasian Flyway?

　Ⓐ The vast majority of the species of birds that use it are water birds.

　Ⓑ More than 490 million birds are believed to use it to migrate each year.

　Ⓒ It covers an area of land that is occupied by four continents.

　Ⓓ There are more than fifty species of waders that are known to use it.

Paragraph 2 is marked with an arrow (⇨).

The East Asian-Australasian Flyway

➡ Every year, numerous species of migratory birds fly south for the winter and then return northward when warmer weather arrives. Billions of birds follow flyways, which are corridors popular with various species and which enable them to visit their breeding grounds and to avoid the extreme temperatures occurring in polar and temperate regions. There are eight major flyways located around the world. One of the longest is the East Asian-Australasian Flyway, which stretches from northern Russia and Alaska into eastern Asia and goes south to Australia and New Zealand.

⇨ The East Asian-Australasian Flyway covers a territory encompassing roughly eighty-five million square kilometers of land and water. There are thirty-seven countries, including the United States, Russia, China, Korea, Japan, India, the Philippines, Indonesia, Australia, and New Zealand, that birds migrate through by using it. Zoologists have thus far identified 492 distinct species of migratory birds that use the flyway and estimate that up to fifty million birds traverse it every year. Most are water birds, including up to eight million of which are birds that ornithologists call waders. These birds primarily reside in shallow water and depend upon marine life forms for sustenance.

*Glossary

ornithologist: a person who studies birds

142

14 Which of the sentences below best expresses the essential information in the highlighted sentence in the passage? Incorrect answer choices change the meaning in important ways or leave out essential information.

The species with the longest migration on the flyway is the bar-tailed godwit, which flies almost 11,000 kilometers over the Pacific Ocean from its breeding grounds in Alaska all the way down to New Zealand.

(A) No bird flies farther over the Pacific Ocean than the bar-tailed godwit, which starts in Alaska and ends up in New Zealand.

(B) The bar-tailed godwit must fly more than 11,000 kilometers to go from Alaska, where it breeds, to New Zealand.

(C) The longest journey is made by the bar-tailed godwit, which starts in Alaska and flies over the Pacific Ocean.

(D) The bar-tailed godwit migrates longer than any other bird on the flyway as it travels from Alaska to New Zealand.

15 According to paragraph 3, how do the majority of birds travel on the East Asian-Australasian Flyway?

(A) By flying their entire journeys without getting any rest

(B) By navigating southward or northward solely over the ocean

(C) By making their journeys in stages consisting of short journeys

(D) By using different routes to their breeding grounds each year

Paragraph 3 is marked with an arrow (➡).

➡ How the birds move along the East Asian-Australasian Flyway depends upon the individual species. Most move in stages by making short flights from one place to another. They often use the same staging areas year after year, so preserving these areas is crucial for the survival of some species. For instance, the lesser sand plover uses the Yellow Sea route through parts of Korea and China and stops at the same places on each stage of its journey. Another species, the whimbrel, annually flies along the same rivers in Russia as it moves north and south. The species with the longest migration on the flyway is the bar-tailed godwit, which flies almost 11,000 kilometers over the Pacific Ocean from its breeding grounds in Alaska all the way down to New Zealand. When it flies back north, it takes a different route as it flies above the Western Pacific Ocean, crosses Korea and Japan, and then moves up the Aleutian Island chain to return to Alaska.

16 In paragraph 4, the author uses "avian botulism and avian influenza" as examples of

(A) illnesses that are fatal to many birds each year

(B) problems that sicken but fail to kill many birds

(C) diseases that many birds spread to other animals

(D) sicknesses that kill more birds than humans do

Paragraph 4 is marked with an arrow (➡).

➡ Among the birds that use the flyway, sixty-four species are considered endangered, and seven are critical, meaning they are nearly extinct. These species—and others—face numerous threats while they migrate. One of the biggest dangers is human hunting. While international agreements that protect the birds and their breeding grounds are making some headway, they do not cover every site. Of the approximately 1,100 sites the birds use in their travels, more than 600 are protected. Of the remainder, 272 are partially protected while the others are unprotected. Another major threat to the birds is the stresses that occur on account of them making such long journeys. These include attacks from predators, the need to acquire food, and the dangers posed by unfavorable weather conditions. Additionally, diseases, particularly avian botulism and avian influenza, take a toll on the birds each year. In 2002 and 2003, a botulism outbreak in Taiwan killed seven percent of the world's black-faced spoonbill population while an outbreak of influenza in China in 2005 decimated an estimated ten percent of the bar-headed geese population.

17 In paragraph 5, the author implies that the land covered by the East Asian-Australasian Flyway

  Ⓐ contains some of the largest urban centers in the world

  Ⓑ is becoming less populated with people in certain areas

  Ⓒ primarily consists of large forests as well as farmland

  Ⓓ is continually undergoing various changes in its appearance

Paragraph 5 is marked with an arrow (➡).

18 The word "stymied" in the passage is closest in meaning to

  Ⓐ hindered

  Ⓑ perceived

  Ⓒ reported

  Ⓓ dismissed

➡ While those issues all pose problems for the birds, the greatest peril they face is that humans will develop their staging areas and breeding grounds. Of all the flyways, the East Asian-Australasian Flyway has the greatest human population, and, as such, the land beneath it is constantly being developed. In China, thirty-seven percent of its intertidal waterways have been lost to land reclamation projects in recent decades. In South Korea, the figure stands at forty-three percent. The spoon-billed sandpiper, which migrates from Russia to Southeast Asia by way of China each year, has lost most of its staging areas since the 1970s. As a result, by 2005, zoologists only counted 350 breeding pairs, which made it a nearly extinct species.

Unfortunately, efforts to stop land reclamation projects have been stymied by the growing pressures of exploding populations and the desires of people to use more land for housing and other projects. In the end, unless people take steps to protect more staging areas, large parts of the East Asian-Australasian Flyway may become empty skies.

*Glossary

intertidal: relating to the water around a shore that is above the low-water mark and beneath the high-water mark

19 Look at the four squares [■] that indicate where the following sentence could be added to the passage.

Among the birds named thusly are storks, and herons, which can be found in abundance in many areas, both northern and southern, or the flyway.

Where would the sentence best fit?

Click on a square [■] to add the sentence to the passage.

The East Asian-Australasian Flyway covers a territory encompassing roughly eighty-five million square kilometers of land and water. There are thirty-seven countries, including the United States, Russia, China, Korea, Japan, India, the Philippines, Indonesia, Australia, and New Zealand, that birds migrate through by using it. **1** Zoologists have thus far identified 492 distinct species of migratory birds that use the flyway and estimate that up to fifty million birds traverse it every year. **2** Most are water birds, including up to eight million of which are birds that ornithologists call waders. **3** These birds primarily reside in shallow water and depend upon marine life forms for sustenance. **4**

*Glossary

ornithologist: a person who studies birds

20 **Directions:** An introductory sentence for a brief summary of the passage is provided below. Complete the summary by selecting the THREE answer choices that express the most important ideas of the passage. Some sentences do not belong because they express ideas that are not presented in the passage or are minor ideas in the passage. **This question is worth 2 points.**

Drag your answer choices to the spaces where they belong. To remove an answer choice, click on it. To review the passage, click on **VIEW TEXT**.

Each year, millions of birds use the East Asian-Australasian Flyway to migrate north and south, but the birds face various dangers as they travel.

-

-

-

ANSWER CHOICES

1   Nearly 500 species of birds totaling roughly fifty million animals use the flyway annually as they migrate to their breeding grounds.

2   The lesser sand plover, whimbrel, and bar-tailed godwit are three of the birds that use various parts of the flyway to migrate.

3   Human hunters kill large numbers of birds at unprotected sites, and many birds on the flyway die after catching various diseases.

4   Because so many places on the flyway are being developed, many sites once used by the birds no longer exist.

5   The East Asian-Australasian Flyway covers an enormous area in countries such as China, the United States, and Russia.

6   Ornithologists have studied the habits of large numbers of birds that migrate to their breeding grounds on the flyway.

Ancient Greek Worship Practices

The Greeks established one of the most advanced societies in ancient times. A highly religious people, they worshiped a large <u>pantheon</u> of gods and goddesses that covered a wide-ranging belief system. Most of these deities were depicted as having human forms and almost always had supernatural abilities. Over time, the Greeks created numerous myths surrounding their deities and came to worship and honor these gods and goddesses in various manners.

According to the Greeks, the major gods and goddesses dwelled on Mount Olympus, where they looked down upon mankind, observed humans' everyday lives, and judged them as they saw fit. Zeus was the supreme leader and controlled the sky, which was symbolized by his ability to cast lightning bolts as weapons. Other gods and goddesses had domain over certain aspects of nature and humanity. Ares was the god of war, Hades ruled the underworld, where the dead went, and Demeter was the goddess of the harvest. In Greek mythology, gods and goddesses frequently became involved in mankind's disputes and interacted with humans in various ways, including falling in love with them and having children with humans.

While the Greeks told myriad stories about their gods and goddesses, they had no all-encompassing tome of religious beliefs such as the Christian Bible. Instead, they possessed a long tradition of religious beliefs and observances passed from generation to generation. Many of these beliefs were based on the notion that the gods would help mankind in return for <u>votive</u> offerings, or gifts, in the guise of sacrifices and donations. The Greeks made requests for assistance from the gods for things humans have asked their deities for throughout history: good harvests, victory in battle, success in business, healing for the sick, and safe journeys. The Greeks normally prayed while standing; they held their hands together, looked up at the sky, and spoke aloud. The worshipers asked for assistance while recounting the good deeds they had done in the name of the deity they were praying to, and they additionally noted how much they had sacrificed for that particular god or goddess. One exception regarded their prayers for the dead. The Greeks firmly believed in the afterlife and thought that the souls of the dead went to the underworld. They performed those prayers by kneeling and looking at the ground during funeral rites.

The Greeks made offerings by visiting sanctuaries dedicated to particular deities. There were shrines for gods and goddesses located both in cities and in rural areas. A typical sanctuary had an enclosing wall surrounding it and sometimes had an elaborate temple. There was an altar upon which worshipers made sacrifices or placed offerings. There was also a stone basin set on a pedestal. It held sacred water used to purify worshipers' hands and was also sprinkled on the offerings made to the deity. Statues of the god or goddess were common as were springs, trees, and other landscape features related to a particular deity. For instance, a temple to Poseidon, the god of the sea, was almost always built near the sea while a temple to Athena, whose tree was the olive, usually had olive trees growing around it.

A typical Greek offering was a ritual slaughter of an animal on an altar. Sheep, goats, cows, and oxen were most commonly used in these sacrifices. The meat of the slaughtered animal was cooked, and the worshipers consumed it; however, the inner organs, such as the heart and liver, were burned rather than eaten as they were reserved for the gods. The Greeks also made offerings of wine, oils, sweets, and other types of food. These sacrifices were often made during religious festivals, so many animals were slaughtered over a period of several days. The ways in which the Greeks celebrated these festivals varied depending upon the geographical location of the events.

The Greeks established colonies throughout the Mediterranean region, so their deities and religious practices became widespread and even took root on the Italian mainland. In later centuries after Rome became powerful, the Romans adopted many of the features of Greek religion and made them their own. This included taking a large number of deities in the Greek pantheon and creating counterparts under different names in the Roman pantheon.

*Glossary

pantheon: all of the gods and goddesses in a particular mythology
votive: offered, given, or performed in accordance with a vow

Beginning

Ancient Greek Worship Practices

➡ The Greeks established one of the most advanced societies in ancient times. A highly religious people, they worshiped a large pantheon of gods and goddesses that covered a wide-ranging belief system. Most of these deities were depicted as having human forms and almost always had supernatural abilities. Over time, the Greeks created numerous myths surrounding their deities and came to worship and honor these gods and goddesses in various manners.

⇨ According to the Greeks, the major gods and goddesses dwelled on Mount Olympus, where they looked down upon mankind, observed humans' everyday lives, and judged them as they saw fit. Zeus was the supreme leader and controlled the sky, which was symbolized by his ability to cast lightning bolts as weapons. Other gods and goddesses had domain over certain aspects of nature and humanity. Ares was the god of war, Hades ruled the underworld, where the dead went, and Demeter was the goddess of the harvest. In Greek mythology, gods and goddesses frequently became involved in mankind's disputes and interacted with humans in various ways, including falling in love with them and having children with humans.

21 According to paragraph 1, which of the following is true about the ancient Greeks?

(A) They created stories about the large number of different deities that they worshiped.

(B) Their belief in various gods and goddesses helped them establish an advance culture.

(C) The deities that they worshiped all had human forms which they could assume.

(D) All of their gods and goddesses were capable of performing various feats of magic.

Paragraph 1 is marked with an arrow (➡).

22 According to paragraph 2, which of the following is NOT true about the Greek gods and goddesses?

(A) Some of them represented various characteristics that humans possessed.

(B) Many of them were said to have become involved in the affairs of humans.

(C) Myths told of how they assumed animal forms and visited the Earth at times.

(D) Greek stories told tales of how some of them had children with humans.

Paragraph 2 is marked with an arrow (⇨).

*Glossary

pantheon: all of the gods and goddesses in a particular mythology

150

23 The word "recounting" in the passage is closest in meaning to

  Ⓐ chanting

  Ⓑ memorizing

  Ⓒ stating

  Ⓓ performing

24 According to paragraph 3, why did the Greeks make sacrifices to the gods?

  Ⓐ They thought the gods would show themselves to the people making sacrifices.

  Ⓑ They considered making sacrifices to be a duty that they had to perform.

  Ⓒ They believed that the gods would reward them by granting their requests.

  Ⓓ They thought it was necessary to keep people from forgetting about the gods.

Paragraph 3 is marked with an arrow (➡).

➡ While the Greeks told myriad stories about their gods and goddesses, they had no all-encompassing tome of religious beliefs such as the Christian Bible. Instead, they possessed a long tradition of religious beliefs and observances passed from generation to generation. Many of these beliefs were based on the notion that the gods would help mankind in return for votive offerings, or gifts, in the guise of sacrifices and donations. The Greeks made requests for assistance from the gods for things humans have asked their deities for throughout history: good harvests, victory in battle, success in business, healing for the sick, and safe journeys. The Greeks normally prayed while standing; they held their hands together, looked up at the sky, and spoke aloud. The worshipers asked for assistance while recounting the good deeds they had done in the name of the deity they were praying to, and they additionally noted how much they had sacrificed for that particular god or goddess. One exception regarded their prayers for the dead. The Greeks firmly believed in the afterlife and thought that the souls of the dead went to the underworld. They performed those prayers by kneeling and looking at the ground during funeral rites.

*Glossary

votive: offered, given, or performed in accordance with a vow

25 The word "elaborate" in the passage is closest in meaning to

- Ⓐ ornate
- Ⓑ rustic
- Ⓒ holy
- Ⓓ traditional

26 In paragraph 4, the author implies that Greek temples

- Ⓐ could sometimes be dedicated to two or more different gods or goddesses
- Ⓑ were much larger in rural areas than they were in urban centers
- Ⓒ had different appearances depending on which god they were dedicated to
- Ⓓ were simple structures that were only used to make sacrifices to deities

Paragraph 4 is marked with an arrow (➡).

27 According to paragraph 5, what did the Greeks do with the inner organs of the animals they sacrificed?

- Ⓐ They cooked and ate them.
- Ⓑ They sacrificed them on the altars.
- Ⓒ They completely burned them.
- Ⓓ They disposed of them during festivals.

Paragraph 5 is marked with an arrow (⇨).

28 Which of the following can be inferred from paragraph 6 about the Romans?

- Ⓐ Their religion resembled the Greeks' religion in many different ways.
- Ⓑ They took many Greek gods as their own after they conquered Greece.
- Ⓒ Their gods and goddesses were more powerful than those of the Greeks.
- Ⓓ The manner in which they worshiped their deities differed from that of the Greeks.

Paragraph 6 is marked with an arrow (➡).

➡ The Greeks made offerings by visiting sanctuaries dedicated to particular deities. There were shrines for gods and goddesses located both in cities and in rural areas. A typical sanctuary had an enclosing wall surrounding it and sometimes had an elaborate temple. There was an altar upon which worshipers made sacrifices or placed offerings. There was also a stone basin set on a pedestal. It held sacred water used to purify worshipers' hands and was also sprinkled on the offerings made to the deity. Statues of the god or goddess were common as were springs, trees, and other landscape features related to a particular deity. For instance, a temple to Poseidon, the god of the sea, was almost always built near the sea while a temple to Athena, whose tree was the olive, usually had olive trees growing around it.

⇨ A typical Greek offering was a ritual slaughter of an animal on an altar. Sheep, goats, cows, and oxen were most commonly used in these sacrifices. The meat of the slaughtered animal was cooked, and the worshipers consumed it; however, the inner organs, such as the heart and liver, were burned rather than eaten as they were reserved for the gods. The Greeks also made offerings of wine, oils, sweets, and other types of food. These sacrifices were often made during religious festivals, so many animals were slaughtered over a period of several days. The ways in which the Greeks celebrated these festivals varied depending upon the geographical location of the events.

➡ The Greeks established colonies throughout the Mediterranean region, so their deities and religious practices became widespread and even took root on the Italian mainland. In later centuries after Rome became powerful, the Romans adopted many of the features of Greek religion and made them their own. This included taking a large number of deities in the Greek pantheon and creating counterparts under different names in the Roman pantheon.

29 Look at the four squares [■] that indicate where the following sentence could be added to the passage.

Additionally, Mercury was the messenger god while Venus was the goddess of love and beauty.

Where would the sentence best fit?

Click on a square [■] to add the sentence to the passage.

According to the Greeks, the major gods and goddesses dwelled on Mount Olympus, where they looked down upon mankind, observed humans' everyday lives, and judged them as they saw fit. Zeus was the supreme leader and controlled the sky, which was symbolized by his ability to cast lightning bolts as weapons. **1** Other gods and goddesses had domain over certain aspects of nature and humanity. **2** Ares was the god of war, Hades ruled the underworld, where the dead went, and Demeter was the goddess of the harvest. **3** In Greek mythology, gods and goddesses frequently became involved in mankind's disputes and interacted with humans in various ways, including falling in love with them and having children with humans. **4**

30 **Directions:** An introductory sentence for a brief summary of the passage is provided below. Complete the summary by selecting the THREE answer choices that express the most important ideas of the passage. Some sentences do not belong because they express ideas that are not presented in the passage or are minor ideas in the passage. **This question is worth 2 points.**

> Drag your answer choices to the spaces where they belong. To remove an answer choice, click on it. To review the passage, click on **VIEW TEXT**.

The Greeks believed in a large number of gods and goddesses, and they had different ways of worshiping them.

-
-
-

ANSWER CHOICES

1. There were temples dedicated to gods and goddesses built only in major cities in Greece.

2. All of the Greek gods and goddesses lived on Mount Olympus, and they often interacted with humans.

3. The Greeks made sacrifices to their deities by slaughtering animals and then burning parts of their bodies.

4. The Greeks often visited sanctuaries dedicated to their deities, and they made different types of prayers at those places.

5. The Romans borrowed a number of deities from the Greek pantheon and made them into Roman gods and goddesses.

6. It was believed by the Greeks that they could gain favor from the gods and goddesses by offering gifts to them.

Actual Test

07

Reading Section Directions

This section measures your ability to understand academic passages in English. You will have **54 minutes** to read and answer questions about **3 passages**. A clock at the top of the screen will show you how much time is remaining.

Most questions are worth 1 point but the last question for each passage is worth more than 1 point. The directions for the last question indicate how many points you may receive.

Some passages include a word or phrase that is underlined. Click on the word or phrase to see a definition or an explanation.

When you want to move to the next question, click on **NEXT**. You may skip questions and go back to them later. If you want to return to previous questions, click on **BACK**. You can click on **REVIEW** at any time, and the review screen will show you which questions you have answered and which you have not answered. From this review screen, you may go directly to any question you have already seen in the Reading section.

Click on **CONTINUE** to go on.

The Byzantine Revival

the church of Hagia Sophia ©Artur Bogacki

The Byzantine Empire lasted from approximately 330 to 1453. During that time, it developed its own unique form of architecture, particularly in the buildings erected in its capital, Constantinople. Centuries after its downfall, there was an architectural movement called the Byzantine Revival, which attempted to emulate the style of buildings from the Byzantine Empire. This period originated in the second half of the nineteenth century and lasted until the early twentieth century. The Byzantine Revival influenced architects and architecture from countries in Western Europe all the way east to Russia, where its primary impact was seen in religious, public, and government buildings rather than those in the private sector.

Byzantine architecture had several unique aspects copied by architects during the period of the Byzantine Revival. The most prominent was the usage of square-based buildings with large central domes surrounded by smaller outlying domes with numerous arches. This design was characteristic of what is arguably the most famous Byzantine structure, the Church of Hagia Sophia, which was built by Emperor Justinian the Great in the sixth century. Russian churches erected during the Byzantine Revival favored this design as many were built with five domes with a large central dome being surrounded by four smaller ones. The Byzantines were further noted for their usage of high vaulted interior ceilings and tall, elaborate columns, both of which were used by architects during the 1800s and 1900s.

It is difficult to determine precisely when the Byzantine Revival originated because Byzantine architectural designs had already been mildly influential in places prior to the nineteenth century. For instance, St. Sophia Cathedral in Pushkin, Russia, located just outside St. Petersburg, was one of the first modern churches constructed with Byzantine influences. Empress Catherine the Great had long desired to make a copy of Hagia Sophia but, on account of the tremendous expenses involved, settled on a smaller design by Scottish architect Charles Cameron. He had worked in Russia for many years and had designed

other works for the empress, but he was not well-schooled in the Byzantine style. The result was a hybrid of Byzantine and Greek styles. His cathedral had a large central dome with four smaller ones, but it also had Doric-style entrances and columns and an unremarkable white-painted exterior. St. Sophia Cathedral was completed in 1788 after six years of construction.

For the next forty years, there was little interest in Byzantine architecture, but then, first in Russia and later in the rest of Europe, it began to gain popularity. Konstantin Thon, the official architect of the Russian imperial court, assisted with the revival when he designed a Byzantine-style church in Moscow. Called the Cathedral of Christ the Savior, it took over four decades to build. Today, it stands more than 100 meters tall and is the tallest Orthodox cathedral in the world. However, the structure was not so impressive to most Russians when it was built since the neoclassical style captivated the Russians at the time. Thus not much else in the Byzantine style was built in Russia for another twenty years. However, in the 1830s and 1840s in Germany, many Byzantine-style churches were constructed in Bavaria. Byzantine architecture became popular elsewhere, so more churches were designed and erected in Denmark and Austria.

By the 1850s, the Byzantine style was favored in Russia, particularly by the monarchy. Though Tsar Nicolas himself disapproved of it, he permitted religious buildings to be constructed in that style. One of the first of these buildings was the Cathedral of Saint Vladimir, which was made in Kiev in 1852. After Nicolas's death in 1855, his son, Tsar Alexander II, made the Byzantine style the official style of the Russian Orthodox Church. His son, Alexander III, endorsed his decision during his reign, which lasted from 1881 to 1894. During the latter half of the nineteenth century, almost 5,000 religious structures with Byzantine influences were built in Russia alone. Unfortunately, many were destroyed during the reign of the communists during Soviet times. Yet other Byzantine Revival buildings were constructed outside Russia. The style was popular in Eastern Europe and even made headway in Great Britain and the United States. In fact, Westminster Cathedral, built between 1895 and 1903, is the most famous Byzantine Revival structure in Great Britain.

*Glossary

vaulted: constructed with an arch that serves as a ceiling

tsar: a king in Russia

1 The word "emulate" in the passage is closest in meaning to

- (A) research
- (B) imitate
- (C) repudiate
- (D) outdo

2 Which of the sentences below best expresses the essential information in the highlighted sentence in the passage? Incorrect answer choices change the meaning in important ways or leave out essential information.

The Byzantine Revival influenced architects and architecture from countries in Western Europe all the way east to Russia, where its primary impact was seen in religious, public, and government buildings rather than those in the private sector.

- (A) Affecting people and buildings in parts of Europe and Russia, the Byzantine Revival was mostly influence in buildings of a religious, public, or government nature.
- (B) Despite the fact that it started in Western Europe, the Byzantine Revival eventually spread to Russia and was used in the design of all kinds of buildings.
- (C) While few private buildings were influenced by the Byzantine Revival, religious, public, and government buildings often resembled those built by the Byzantines.
- (D) Many architects were influenced during the Byzantine Revival, so their influence started in Russia and then moved on to various countries in Western Europe.

The Byzantine Revival

The Byzantine Empire lasted from approximately 330 to 1453. During that time, it developed its own unique form of architecture, particularly in the buildings erected in its capital, Constantinople. Centuries after its downfall, there was an architectural movement called the Byzantine Revival, which attempted to emulate the style of buildings from the Byzantine Empire. This period originated in the second half of the nineteenth century and lasted until the early twentieth century. The Byzantine Revival influenced architects and architecture from countries in Western Europe all the way east to Russia, where its primary impact was seen in religious, public, and government buildings rather than those in the private sector.

3 The author discusses "the Church of Hagia Sophia" in order to

(A) note how its design affected the construction of churches throughout Europe

(B) point out how one of its most notable features influenced the Byzantine Revival

(C) describe why Emperor Justinian the Great had it designed in a certain manner

(D) claim that its design was solely responsible for the onset of the Byzantine Revival

4 Which of the following can be inferred from paragraph 2 about Byzantine Revival architects?

(A) Many of them went to Greece or other areas influenced by the Byzantine Empire to be trained.

(B) The works that they designed were frequently disliked by many members of the public.

(C) They preferred to use multiple domes on their buildings more often than tall columns.

(D) It was common for them to speak Greek since they were interested in Byzantine architecture.

Paragraph 2 is marked with an arrow (➡).

5 According to paragraph 3, St. Sophia Cathedral was built smaller than originally planned because

(A) making it much larger would have been too expensive

(B) the Russians lacked enough material to increase its size

(C) the architect was unable to design a cathedral bigger than it

(D) a bigger cathedral would have been structurally unsafe

Paragraph 3 is marked with an arrow (⇨).

➡ Byzantine architecture had several unique aspects copied by architects during the period of the Byzantine Revival. The most prominent was the usage of square-based buildings with large central domes surrounded by smaller outlying domes with numerous arches. This design was characteristic of what is arguably the most famous Byzantine structure, the Church of Hagia Sophia, which was built by Emperor Justinian the Great in the sixth century. Russian churches erected during the Byzantine Revival favored this design as many were built with five domes with a large central dome being surrounded by four smaller ones. The Byzantines were further noted for their usage of high vaulted interior ceilings and tall, elaborate columns, both of which were used by architects during the 1800s and 1900s.

⇨ It is difficult to determine precisely when the Byzantine Revival originated because Byzantine architectural designs had already been mildly influential in places prior to the nineteenth century. For instance, St. Sophia Cathedral in Pushkin, Russia, located just outside St. Petersburg, was one of the first modern churches constructed with Byzantine influences. Empress Catherine the Great had long desired to make a copy of Hagia Sophia but, on account of the tremendous expenses involved, settled on a smaller design by Scottish architect Charles Cameron. He had worked in Russia for many years and had designed other works for the empress, but he was not well-schooled in the Byzantine style. The result was a hybrid of Byzantine and Greek styles. His cathedral had a large central dome with four smaller ones, but it also had Doric-style entrances and columns and an unremarkable white-painted exterior. St. Sophia Cathedral was completed in 1788 after six years of construction.

*Glossary

vaulted: constructed with an arch that serves as a ceiling

160

6 According to paragraph 4, what happened in the mid-1800s?

(A) Architects in Denmark and Austria started outperforming those in Russia and Germany.

(B) A large number of Byzantine Revival cathedrals were built in Moscow.

(C) The Byzantine style of architecture became popular in parts of Germany.

(D) Architects traveled to Bavaria to see the Byzantine-style buildings constructed there.

Paragraph 4 is marked with an arrow (➡).

➡ For the next forty years, there was little interest in Byzantine architecture, but then, first in Russia and later in the rest of Europe, it began to gain popularity. Konstantin Thon, the official architect of the Russian imperial court, assisted with the revival when he designed a Byzantine-style church in Moscow. Called the Cathedral of Christ the Savior, it took over four decades to build. Today, it stands more than 100 meters tall and is the tallest Orthodox cathedral in the world. However, the structure was not so impressive to most Russians when it was built since the neoclassical style captivated the Russians at the time. Thus not much else in the Byzantine style was built in Russia for another twenty years. However, in the 1830s and 1840s in Germany, many Byzantine-style churches were constructed in Bavaria. Byzantine architecture became popular elsewhere, so more churches were designed and erected in Denmark and Austria.

7 The word "endorsed" in the passage is closest in meaning to

(A) recommended

(B) proposed

(C) reversed

(D) prohibited

8 In paragraph 5, the author's description of the Byzantine Revival mentions all of the following EXCEPT:

(A) what the Soviets did to many Byzantine Revival religious structures after they were built

(B) the reason that architects stopped designing buildings in the style of the Byzantines

(C) some of the nations other than Russia in which the Byzantine Revival took place

(D) the way in which some Russian tsars enabled the Byzantine Revival to thrive in Russia

Paragraph 5 is marked with an arrow (➡).

➡ By the 1850s, the Byzantine style was favored in Russia, particularly by the monarchy. Though Tsar Nicolas himself disapproved of it, he permitted religious buildings to be constructed in that style. One of the first of these buildings was the Cathedral of Saint Vladimir, which was made in Kiev in 1852. After Nicolas's death in 1855, his son, Tsar Alexander II, made the Byzantine style the official style of the Russian Orthodox Church. His son, Alexander III, endorsed his decision during his reign, which lasted from 1881 to 1894. During the latter half of the nineteenth century, almost 5,000 religious structures with Byzantine influences were built in Russia alone. Unfortunately, many were destroyed during the reign of the communists during Soviet times. Yet other Byzantine Revival buildings were constructed outside Russia. The style was popular in Eastern Europe and even made headway in Great Britain and the United States. In fact, Westminster Cathedral, built between 1895 and 1903, is the most famous Byzantine Revival structure in Great Britain.

*Glossary

tsar: a king in Russia

9   Look at the four squares [■] that indicate where the following sentence could be added to the passage.

This can be attributed to the fact that historical interest in the Byzantine Empire remained high centuries after its downfall.

Where would the sentence best fit?

Click on a square [■] to add the sentence to the passage.

It is difficult to determine precisely when the Byzantine Revival originated because Byzantine architectural designs had already been mildly influential in places prior to the nineteenth century. **1** For instance, St. Sophia Cathedral in Pushkin, Russia, located just outside St. Petersburg, was one of the first modern churches constructed with Byzantine influences. **2** Empress Catherine the Great had long desired to make a copy of Hagia Sophia but, on account of the tremendous expenses involved, settled on a smaller design by Scottish architect Charles Cameron. **3** He had worked in Russia for many years and had designed other works for the empress, but he was not well-schooled in the Byzantine style. **4** The result was a hybrid of Byzantine and Greek styles. His cathedral had a large central dome with four smaller ones, but it also had Doric-style entrances and columns and an unremarkable white-painted exterior. St. Sophia Cathedral was completed in 1788 after six years of construction.

10 Directions: An introductory sentence for a brief summary of the passage is provided below. Complete the summary by selecting the THREE answer choices that express the most important ideas of the passage. Some sentences do not belong because they express ideas that are not presented in the passage or are minor ideas in the passage. **This question is worth 2 points.**

> Drag your answer choices to the spaces where they belong. To remove an answer choice, click on it. To review the passage, click on **VIEW TEXT**.

The Byzantine Revival was a period when architects in many countries attempted to recreate various aspects of architecture from the Byzantine Empire.

-
-
-

ANSWER CHOICES

1. Architects such as Charles Cameron and Konstantin Thon contributed to the popularization of Byzantine architecture.

2. While the Byzantine Revival was highly popular in Russia, it also spread to countries such as Germany, Great Britain, and the United States.

3. St. Sophia Cathedral was originally intended to be a copy of Hagia Sophia, but it was made to be somewhat smaller than the building in Constantinople.

4. Multiple domes, square-shaped buildings, and indoor vaulted ceilings were all aspects of Byzantine architecture that later architects used.

5. The Byzantine Revival came to an end in the nineteenth century when other forms of architecture became more prominent.

6. The Byzantine Empire lasted for more than 1,000 years, and it developed a distinctive form of architecture during that time.

Milankovitch Cycles and Ice Ages

The Earth periodically endures ice ages lasting millions of years. They are not continual periods of cold though as glaciers sometimes advance toward the equator yet retreat toward the poles on other occasions. Many attempts have been made to explain why glaciers behave in this manner, but arguably the best explanation is the theory of Milankovitch Cycles.

Milutin Milankovitch was a Serbian mathematician, engineer, and climatologist who, between the years 1912 and 1917, published several papers explaining his work on the theory that bears his name. According to Milankovitch, there are three cycles—called eccentricity, obliquity, and precession—which are based on different properties of Earth's rotation around the sun and variations in the tilt of Earth's axis. Due to the discrepancies they cause in the position of Earth in relation to the sun, different parts of the planet receive varying amounts of solar radiation at certain times of the year. Over long periods of time, patterns emerge that, in Milankovitch's opinion, explained the cyclical nature of the planet's ice ages.

The first cycle is related to the eccentricity of Earth's orbit around the sun. If its orbit were a perfect circle, its eccentricity would be zero; however, it is not circular but fluctuates between its closest approach to the sun—perihelion—and its farthest approach—aphelion. Eccentricity is the measure of the difference between them and a perfect orbit. Earth's eccentricity varies from a minimum of 0.0005 outside a circular orbit at perihelion to a maximum of 0.0607 at aphelion and changes over a 100,000-year period. Currently, Earth's eccentricity is around 0.017, which means its orbit is closer to the perihelion point than the aphelion one. Even so, Earth currently receives less solar radiation than it would at the perihelion point.

Yet by itself, this variation in the planet's distance from the sun could not entirely explain the cyclical nature of ice ages. The obliquity of the planet therefore additionally plays an important role. Obliquity refers to the angle at which Earth's axis is tilted related to the plane of its orbit around the sun. It is the reason the areas closer to the poles experience four seasons as temperatures vary with the amount of solar radiation striking the planet in these places. Earth's obliquity changes during a roughly 40,000-year cycle from a minimum of 22.1 degrees to a maximum tilt of 24.5 degrees. At present, the tilt is around 23.5 degrees. According to Milankovitch's theory, the larger the tilt, the greater the differences in seasonal temperatures.

The third cycle of the theory is precession and is best explained by imagining that Earth is like a child's toy top that is spinning. However, the spinning is reaching its end, so the top is beginning to wobble. Earth acts similarly, but, unlike a top, it never ceases swaying, and it vibrates in the same pattern every 26,000 years. This cycle causes Earth's axis to point in different directions over that period of time. At present, the axis is pointing toward Polaris, the North Star. The variations are the result of the effects of the sun's and moon's gravity on the planet. Precession is important because it changes the way Earth is

tilted toward the sun at perihelion and aphelion. At present, this means the Northern Hemisphere is tilted away from the sun when it is at perihelion, so, somewhat <u>ironically</u>, the Northern Hemisphere experiences winter when Earth is closest to the sun.

In creating his theory, Milankovitch attempted to explain why periodic ice ages occurred. He believed that if all three cycles combine to place Earth in a position where the Northern Hemisphere experiences prolonged winter weather at much lower temperatures due to a significant drop in the amount of solar radiation it receives, then an ice age occurs. His hypothesis is accepted by many experts, but there is opposition to it. The main argument against it is that there is insufficient data from past climate events to support the theory. There is also evidence that major glacial events occurred when the Northern Hemisphere was positioned so that it received plenty of solar radiation. Hence it is possible that while Milankovitch Cycles may explain why some ice ages happened, other undiscovered factors may have caused additional ones to take place.

*Glossary

eccentricity: a deviation from a periodic or orbital path

ironically: relating to the usage of words to have a meaning that is the opposite of the literal meaning of the words

Beginning

Milankovitch Cycles and Ice Ages

➡ The Earth periodically endures ice ages lasting millions of years. They are not continual periods of cold though as glaciers sometimes advance toward the equator yet retreat toward the poles on other occasions. Many attempts have been made to explain why glaciers behave in this manner, but arguably the best explanation is the theory of Milankovitch Cycles.

Milutin Milankovitch was a Serbian mathematician, engineer, and climatologist who, between the years 1912 and 1917, published several papers explaining his work on the theory that bears his name. According to Milankovitch, there are three cycles—called eccentricity, obliquity, and precession—which are based on different properties of Earth's rotation around the sun and variations in the tilt of Earth's axis. Due to the discrepancies they cause in the position of Earth in relation to the sun, different parts of the planet receive varying amounts of solar radiation at certain times of the year. Over long periods of time, patterns emerge that, in Milankovitch's opinion, explained the cyclical nature of the planet's ice ages.

11 According to paragraph 1, which of the following is true about ice ages?

   Ⓐ They have happened only a couple of times in the history of the Earth.

   Ⓑ The sizes of the areas covered by glaciers vary at different times during them.

   Ⓒ They typically come to a conclusion a few thousand years after they begin.

   Ⓓ There are several theories that are accepted regarding why they take place.

Paragraph 1 is marked with an arrow (➡).

12 The word "discrepancies" in the passage is closest in meaning to

   Ⓐ redundancies

   Ⓑ inconsistencies

   Ⓒ similarities

   Ⓓ appearances

*Glossary

eccentricity: a deviation from a periodic or orbital path

More Available ▲

13 The word "fluctuates" in the passage is closest in meaning to

(A) nears

(B) revolves

(C) remains

(D) alters

14 According to paragraph 4, what is the obliquity of Earth?

(A) The difference in how much and how little it tilts

(B) The angle at which the planet is tilted on its axis

(C) The effect its tilting has on solar radiation hitting the planet

(D) The rate at which it changes the amount it tilts

Paragraph 4 is marked with an arrow (➡).

The first cycle is related to the eccentricity of Earth's orbit around the sun. If its orbit were a perfect circle, its eccentricity would be zero; however, it is not circular but fluctuates between its closest approach to the sun—perihelion—and its farthest approach—aphelion. Eccentricity is the measure of the difference between them and a perfect orbit. Earth's eccentricity varies from a minimum of 0.0005 outside a circular orbit at perihelion to a maximum of 0.0607 at aphelion and changes over a 100,000-year period. Currently, Earth's eccentricity is around 0.017, which means its orbit is closer to the perihelion point than the aphelion one. Even so, Earth currently receives less solar radiation than it would at the perihelion point.

➡ Yet by itself, this variation in the planet's distance from the sun could not entirely explain the cyclical nature of ice ages. The obliquity of the planet therefore additionally plays an important role. Obliquity refers to the angle at which Earth's axis is tilted related to the plane of its orbit around the sun. It is the reason the areas closer to the poles experience four seasons as temperatures vary with the amount of solar radiation striking the planet in these places. Earth's obliquity changes during a roughly 40,000-year cycle from a minimum of 22.1 degrees to a maximum tilt of 24.5 degrees. At present, the tilt is around 23.5 degrees. According to Milankovitch's theory, the larger the tilt, the greater the differences in seasonal temperatures.

More Available

15 In paragraph 5, why does the author mention "a child's toy top"?

(A) To prove that the rotation of Earth sometimes slows down

(B) To explain the concept of the eccentricity of Earth

(C) To make a comparison between how it and Earth behaves

(D) To show that it is possible to predict when ice ages will occur

Paragraph 5 is marked with an arrow (➡).

16 In paragraph 5, all of the following questions are answered EXCEPT:

(A) Why does the Northern Hemisphere experience winter despite being closest to the sun during that season?

(B) What causes Earth's axis to point in different directions over a period lasting thousands of years?

(C) What is the name of the heavenly body at which Earth's axis is currently directed toward?

(D) When is the current 26,000 year cycle that Earth is in going to come to its conclusion?

Paragraph 5 is marked with an arrow (➡).

➡ The third cycle of the theory is precession and is best explained by imagining that Earth is like a child's toy top that is spinning. However, the spinning is reaching its end, so the top is beginning to wobble. Earth acts similarly, but, unlike a top, it never ceases swaying, and it vibrates in the same pattern every 26,000 years. This cycle causes Earth's axis to point in different directions over that period of time. At present, the axis is pointing toward Polaris, the North Star. The variations are the result of the effects of the sun's and moon's gravity on the planet. Precession is important because it changes the way Earth is tilted toward the sun at perihelion and aphelion. At present, this means the Northern Hemisphere is tilted away from the sun when it is at perihelion, so, somewhat ironically, the Northern Hemisphere experiences winter when Earth is closest to the sun.

*Glossary

ironically: relating to the usage of words to have a meaning that is the opposite of the literal meaning of the words

17 The word "ones" in the passage refers to

(A) insufficient data

(B) Milankovitch Cycles

(C) some ice ages

(D) other undiscovered factors

18 According to paragraph 6, some scientists oppose the theory of Milankovitch Cycles because

(A) they believe solar radiation has a minor effect on causing ice ages

(B) they claim that the Earth is currently not in an ice age

(C) they support other theories that they state are easier to verify

(D) they lack enough evidence from prior ice ages to prove the theory

Paragraph 6 is marked with an arrow (➡).

➡ In creating his theory, Milankovitch attempted to explain why periodic ice ages occurred. He believed that if all three cycles combine to place Earth in a position where the Northern Hemisphere experiences prolonged winter weather at much lower temperatures due to a significant drop in the amount of solar radiation it receives, then an ice age occurs. His hypothesis is accepted by many experts, but there is opposition to it. The main argument against it is that there is insufficient data from past climate events to support the theory. There is also evidence that major glacial events occurred when the Northern Hemisphere was positioned so that it received plenty of solar radiation. Hence it is possible that while Milankovitch Cycles may explain why some ice ages happened, other undiscovered factors may have caused additional ones to take place.

Q
REVIEW

?
HELP

‹
BACK

›
NEXT

HIDE TIME 00:54:00

More Available ▲

19 Look at the four squares [■] that indicate where the following sentence could be added to the passage.

For instance, the Northern Hemisphere is tilted away from the sun during winter and toward the sun in summer.

Where would the sentence best fit?

Click on a square [■] to add the sentence to the passage.

Yet by itself, this variation in the planet's distance from the sun could not entirely explain the cyclical nature of ice ages. The obliquity of the planet therefore additionally plays an important role. Obliquity refers to the angle at which Earth's axis is tilted related to the plane of its orbit around the sun. **1** It is the reason the areas closer to the poles experience four seasons as temperatures vary with the amount of solar radiation striking the planet in these places. **2** Earth's obliquity changes during a roughly 40,000-year cycle from a minimum of 22.1 degrees to a maximum tilt of 24.5 degrees. **3** At present, the tilt is around 23.5 degrees. **4** According to Milankovitch's theory, the larger the tilt, the greater the differences in seasonal temperatures.

20 Directions: Select the appropriate statements from the answer choices and match them to the part of the Milankovitch Cycle to which they relate. TWO of the answer choices will NOT be used. **This question is worth 4 points.**

Drag your answer choices to the spaces where they belong. To remove an answer choice, click on it. To review the passage, click on **VIEW TEXT**.

ANSWER CHOICES

1 Is caused by a pattern of swaying that repeats every 26,000 years

2 Has the greatest effect of the three cycles on the occurring of ice ages

3 Can be described by pointing out its similarities to a spinning top

4 Causes there to be four seasons on certain parts of the planet

5 Concerns the distance Earth is from the sun as it orbits the star

6 Happens on account of the gravity of the sun and the moon

7 Results in ice ages in the Southern Hemisphere rather than in the Northern Hemisphere

8 Can lead to great differences in the temperatures of the seasons

9 Is currently at a position closer to perihelion than it is to aphelion

PART OF THE MILANKOVITCH CYCLE

Eccentricity (Select 2)

-
-

Obliquity (Select 2)

-
-

Procession (Select 3)

-
-
-

Hellenism and Alexandria

Between 334 and 323 B.C., Alexander the Great conquered much of the land covering the modern-day Middle East. As his armies marched from Greece through this territory, his soldiers and civilian administrators spread Greek culture, which is commonly referred to as Hellenism. The Hellenistic expansion reached its acme with Alexander's founding of the city of Alexandria, which was located in Egypt and which proceeded to become among the ancient world's greatest and most influential cities.

Alexander designed and initiated construction on the city bearing his name in 331 B.C. Nevertheless, by the time Alexandria was completed, he had already moved on to conquer other lands. When Alexander died in 323 B.C., his successors divided his vast empire amongst themselves. Ptolemy, one of Alexander's generals, became the leader of Egypt. On his deathbed, Alexander had selected Egypt as the site of his final resting place, so serving as the guardian of Alexander's tomb greatly enhanced Ptolemy's prestige. This additionally set the stage for Alexandria to become the center of Hellenism in the Mediterranean world.

Unfortunately, Ptolemy and the other successors to Alexander's empire soon began squabbling, resulting in war. During the fighting, Ptolemy expanded his domains into southern Syria, Cyprus, the Aegean Sea, and the Greek mainland. By 306 B.C., he had declared himself Pharaoh Ptolemy the First and established his royal household and seat of power in Alexandria. From there, he ruled until his death at the age of eighty-four in 283 B.C., and then his son—also named Ptolemy—succeeded him. Ptolemy the First and his successors ruled Egypt for nearly 300 years, and during that time, they transformed Alexandria into a showcase of Greek culture. Within a century of its founding, Alexandria had become the second largest city in the Mediterranean world. It became the center of trade in the Eastern Mediterranean, so it grew wealthy and expanded. While Alexandria eventually had large populations of Jews and Egyptians, its rulers ensured that the Greek community dominated all aspects of life there.

Alexandria was noted as a trading port and was also the intellectual center of the ancient Greek world, which was mostly the result of the construction of a great library around 300 B.C. Ptolemy ordered that <u>scrolls</u> and books from everywhere in the known world be gathered at the Library of Alexandria. Eventually, the collection became the largest in the world and numbered nearly 700,000 items. The librarians decreed that no scroll or book could be placed in the library unless it was first translated into Greek. Therefore, numerous Egyptian works were translated, and a great amount of knowledge spread. Over time, Alexandria became the one place in the Mediterranean world that every scholar in ancient times desired to visit.

Ptolemy the First further enhanced his standing as Alexander's successor by creating a cult of Alexander. While still alive, Alexander had visited an <u>oracle</u> in Egypt and had been advised that he was a

son of the Greek god Zeus. Believing that, Alexander acted as though he were a god and was accordingly revered as a deity both while alive and dead. Ptolemy turned this to his advantage by securing Alexander's body in a tomb in Alexandria. He transformed it into a tourist attraction and established a cult of Alexander to perpetuate the notion of the deceased conqueror as a god. The cult attracted vast numbers of visitors and further heightened Alexandria's standing as the center of Hellenism.

Despite being a stronghold of Hellenism, the Ptolemaic rulers understood that Egypt was not Greece, so they made concessions to the natives to maintain peace in their land. Resultantly, they never forced the Greek language, religion, or culture on the Egyptian people; however, any native Egyptian desiring to rise in power and influence in the Ptolemaic bureaucracy was obligated to learn the Greek language and to adopt Greek customs. Ultimately, despite 300 years of Greek rule, the people of Egypt maintained many of their historic traditions, religious aspects, and language. When Ptolemaic rule of Egypt came to its conclusion after the Roman general Octavian conquered Alexandria and the land around it in 31 B.C., Ptolemaic rule of Egypt ceased, and so did most of the influence of Hellenism in Alexandria.

*Glossary

scroll: a roll of parchment or other material upon which there is writing

oracle: a person who is believed to be able to tell the future

Beginning

Hellenism and Alexandria

➡ Between 334 and 323 B.C., Alexander the Great conquered much of the land covering the modern-day Middle East. As his armies marched from Greece through this territory, his soldiers and civilian administrators spread Greek culture, which is commonly referred to as Hellenism. The Hellenistic expansion reached its acme with Alexander's founding of the city of Alexandria, which was located in Egypt and which proceeded to become among the ancient world's greatest and most influential cities.

21 The author discusses "Alexander the Great" in paragraph 1 in order to

(A) note how he emphasized the spread of Hellenism in the ancient world

(B) mention the lands that he conquered during all of his wars

(C) point out some of the great military victories that he achieved

(D) describe his role in the spreading of Hellenism in various places

Paragraph 1 is marked with an arrow (➡).

22 The word "acme" in the passage is closest in meaning to

(A) height

(B) oversight

(C) conclusion

(D) influence

23 The word "squabbling" in the passage is closest in meaning to

Ⓐ dividing

Ⓑ skirmishing

Ⓒ contending

Ⓓ arguing

24 According to paragraphs 2 and 3, which of the following is NOT true about Ptolemy?

Ⓐ He gained more territory for himself in the two decades after Alexander the Great's death.

Ⓑ He ruled his land from Alexandria and was the pharaoh there until 283 B.C.

Ⓒ He started a dynasty based in Alexandria that would last for more than four centuries.

Ⓓ He took control of Egypt following the death of Alexander the Great.

Paragraphs 2 and 3 are marked with arrows (➡) and (⇨).

25 According to paragraph 3, Alexandria became a rich city because

Ⓐ the Jews and Egyptians that lived there were highly successful at business ventures

Ⓑ its geographical location at the mouth of the Nile River made it a trading hub

Ⓒ it served as one of the main trading centers in the eastern part of the Mediterranean Sea

Ⓓ the Greeks maintained strict control of the city as opposed to the Egyptians

Paragraph 3 is marked with an arrow (⇨).

➡ Alexander designed and initiated construction on the city bearing his name in 331 B.C. Nevertheless, by the time Alexandria was completed, he had already moved on to conquer other lands. When Alexander died in 323 B.C., his successors divided his vast empire amongst themselves. Ptolemy, one of Alexander's generals, became the leader of Egypt. On his deathbed, Alexander had selected Egypt as the site of his final resting place, so serving as the guardian of Alexander's tomb greatly enhanced Ptolemy's prestige. This additionally set the stage for Alexandria to become the center of Hellenism in the Mediterranean world.

⇨ Unfortunately, Ptolemy and the other successors to Alexander's empire soon began squabbling, resulting in war. During the fighting, Ptolemy expanded his domains into southern Syria, Cyprus, the Aegean Sea, and the Greek mainland. By 306 B.C., he had declared himself Pharaoh Ptolemy the First and established his royal household and seat of power in Alexandria. From there, he ruled until his death at the age of eighty-four in 283 B.C., and then his son—also named Ptolemy—succeeded him. Ptolemy the First and his successors ruled Egypt for nearly 300 years, and during that time, they transformed Alexandria into a showcase of Greek culture. Within a century of its founding, Alexandria had become the second largest city in the Mediterranean world. It became the center of trade in the Eastern Mediterranean, so it grew wealthy and expanded. While Alexandria eventually had large populations of Jews and Egyptians, its rulers ensured that the Greek community dominated all aspects of life there.

REVIEW

HELP

BACK

NEXT

HIDE TIME 00:54:00

More Available

26 In paragraph 4, the author suggests that the Library of Alexandria

Ⓐ was the largest physical structure created during ancient times

Ⓑ contained works that were written in a variety of languages

Ⓒ started its own school that trained scholars in certain subjects

Ⓓ had the most complete collection of works from Greece in the ancient world

Paragraph 4 is marked with an arrow (➡).

27 According to paragraph 5, which of the following is true about the cult of Alexander?

Ⓐ Its members were the first to declare that Alexander the Great was a god.

Ⓑ It was responsible for increasing the number of tourists going to Alexandria.

Ⓒ The followers of it established temples to Alexander the Great in some cities.

Ⓓ Some of the cult members kept the tomb of Alexander the Great from harm.

Paragraph 5 is marked with an arrow (⇨).

➡ Alexandria was noted as a trading port and was also the intellectual center of the ancient Greek world, which was mostly the result of the construction of a great library around 300 B.C. Ptolemy ordered that scrolls and books from everywhere in the known world be gathered at the Library of Alexandria. Eventually, the collection became the largest in the world and numbered nearly 700,000 items. The librarians decreed that no scroll or book could be placed in the library unless it was first translated into Greek. Therefore, numerous Egyptian works were translated, and a great amount of knowledge spread. Over time, Alexandria became the one place in the Mediterranean world that every scholar in ancient times desired to visit.

⇨ Ptolemy the First further enhanced his standing as Alexander's successor by creating a cult of Alexander. While still alive, Alexander had visited an oracle in Egypt and had been advised that he was a son of the Greek god Zeus. Believing that, Alexander acted as though he were a god and was accordingly revered as a deity both while alive and dead. Ptolemy turned this to his advantage by securing Alexander's body in a tomb in Alexandria. He transformed it into a tourist attraction and established a cult of Alexander to perpetuate the notion of the deceased conqueror as a god. The cult attracted vast numbers of visitors and further heightened Alexandria's standing as the center of Hellenism.

*Glossary

scroll: a roll of parchment or other material upon which there is writing

oracle: a person who is believed to be able to tell the future

28 According to paragraph 6, an Egyptian wanting to work in the bureaucracy in Alexandria had to

Ⓐ denounce the ways of ancient Egypt and follow the ways of the Greeks

Ⓑ worship the same gods and goddesses that the Greeks did

Ⓒ prove that he could be loyal to the Greeks that were higher above him

Ⓓ follow the same customs as the Greeks and also speak the Greek language

Paragraph 6 is marked with an arrow (➡).

➡ Despite being a stronghold of Hellenism, the Ptolemaic rulers understood that Egypt was not Greece, so they made concessions to the natives to maintain peace in their land. Resultantly, they never forced the Greek language, religion, or culture on the Egyptian people; however, any native Egyptian desiring to rise in power and influence in the Ptolemaic bureaucracy was obligated to learn the Greek language and to adopt Greek customs. Ultimately, despite 300 years of Greek rule, the people of Egypt maintained many of their historic traditions, religious aspects, and language. When Ptolemaic rule of Egypt came to its conclusion after the Roman general Octavian conquered Alexandria and the land around it in 31 B.C., Ptolemaic rule of Egypt ceased, and so did most of the influence of Hellenism in Alexandria.

29 Look at the four squares [■] that indicate where the following sentence could be added to the passage.

Only Rome, which was located across the Mediterranean Sea on the Italian peninsula, had a greater population.

Where would the sentence best fit?

Click on a square [■] to add the sentence to the passage.

Unfortunately, Ptolemy and the other successors to Alexander's empire soon began squabbling, which resulted in war. During the fighting, Ptolemy expanded his domains into southern Syria, Cyprus, the Aegean Sea, and the Greek mainland. By 306 B.C., he had declared himself Pharaoh Ptolemy the First and established his royal household and seat of power in Alexandria. **1** From there, he ruled until his death at the age of eighty-four in 283 B.C., and then his son—also named Ptolemy—succeeded him. **2** Ptolemy the First and his successors ruled Egypt for nearly 300 years, and during that time, they transformed Alexandria into a showcase of Greek culture. **3** Within a century of its founding, Alexandria had become the second largest city in the Mediterranean world. **4** It became the center of trade in the Eastern Mediterranean, so it grew wealthy and expanded. While Alexandria eventually had large populations of Jews and Egyptians, its rulers ensured that the Greek community dominated all aspects of life in there.

30 **Directions:** An introductory sentence for a brief summary of the passage is provided below. Complete the summary by selecting the THREE answer choices that express the most important ideas of the passage. Some sentences do not belong because they express ideas that are not presented in the passage or are minor ideas in the passage. **This question is worth 2 points.**

Drag your answer choices to the spaces where they belong. To remove an answer choice, click on it. To review the passage, click on **VIEW TEXT**.

The city of Alexandria, Egypt, was established by Alexander the Great and served as a center of Hellenism for three centuries.

-
-
-

ANSWER CHOICES

1. When the Roman Octavian captured Alexandria in 31 B.C., the Greek influence of Alexandria decreased tremendously.

2. Alexander the Great conquered a great deal of the known world in a period lasting roughly eleven years.

3. The Greek general Ptolemy ruled his empire from Alexandria but failed to start a long-lasting dynasty.

4. The cult of Alexander the Great was centered in Alexandria and attracted many people to the city to visit the tomb of Alexander the Great.

5. Scholars from around the Mediterranean went to Alexandria in order to study the manuscripts kept at the Library of Alexandria.

6. Alexandria was a powerful trading center in the Mediterranean area and became a wealthy city because of that trade.

Actual Test

08

Reading Section Directions

This section measures your ability to understand academic passages in English. You will have **54 minutes** to read and answer questions about **3 passages**. A clock at the top of the screen will show you how much time is remaining.

Most questions are worth 1 point but the last question for each passage is worth more than 1 point. The directions for the last question indicate how many points you may receive.

Some passages include a word or phrase that is <u>underlined</u>. Click on the word or phrase to see a definition or an explanation.

When you want to move to the next question, click on **NEXT**. You may skip questions and go back to them later. If you want to return to previous questions, click on **BACK**. You can click on **REVIEW** at any time, and the review screen will show you which questions you have answered and which you have not answered. From this review screen, you may go directly to any question you have already seen in the Reading section.

Click on **CONTINUE** to go on.

The Hajnal Line

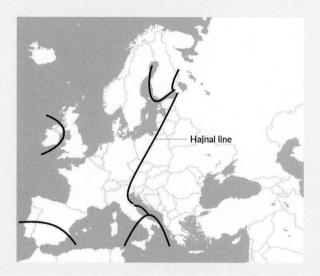

Hajnal line

There are myriad differences between Western and Eastern Europe, including obvious ones related to language, culture, and history. One that may not be apparent at first glance is related to marriage and birthrates. In 1965, Hungarian economist John Hajnal published a paper claiming Europe could be divided into two distinct regions. The article proposed that an imaginary line, now called the Hajnal Line, running from Saint Petersburg, Russia, to Trieste, Italy, separated two highly different regions of Europe based upon marriage and birth statistics. The primary thrust of Hajnal's report was that in Western Europe, people married later in age and had fewer children than people in Eastern Europe did. It also pointed out there were weaker family ties between parents and children in Western Europe than in Eastern Europe.

Throughout European history, the age of marriage has varied greatly. But as far back as Roman times, historical records show that men and women in Western Europe typically got married in their early twenties as opposed to people in Eastern European regions, where they more commonly married in their late teens. In Western Europe, the historic average age of marriage for women was twenty-four, and it was twenty-six for men. Roughly ten percent of the population never married, and, in some cases, such as after being widowed or divorced, people married a second time. Hajnal also detected a considerable lag between the time women were capable of having children and actually giving birth. The average age when most women are able to give birth is fourteen. With Western European women getting married at the average age of twenty-four, many of their childbearing years went unutilized. Coupled with some people never marrying and a strict taboo on birth out of wedlock, the result was a lower birthrate in comparison to Eastern Europe.

Not every place west of the Hajnal Line fits that pattern though. Ireland, Finland, and parts of southern

Italy and southern Spain have seen historically higher marriage rates, earlier marriages, and higher birthrates than other regions in Western Europe. Nevertheless, these were not consistent. For instance, birthrates in these regions fluctuated according to economic conditions. In Ireland, after the Irish Potato Famine in the late 1840s, birthrates declined considerably for several years as people married later and had fewer children because they feared the consequences if famine returned.

Economic stability also played a contributing role in the lower marriage rates and birthrates in most of Western Europe. With a better quality of life compared to those living in Eastern Europe, Western European families normally had better medical care and access to steady food supplies. This resulted in lower overall death rates and child mortality rates. Therefore, there was less emphasis on getting married early and having large families. Meanwhile, in Eastern Europe, where periodic waves of disease, famine, and war took their toll on human life, people felt a stronger urge to marry early, to start having children, and to have enough children to replace those who frequently lost their lives during childbirth or in their infancy.

Religious reasons for the differences in marriage rates and birthrates have been proven to have had little bearing on the matter. Virtually all of Europe was Christian in one form or another for the last few centuries. While Christianity advocates marriage and starting families, it is not an obligation, nor are those who fail to do so ostracized from society.

One additional factor affecting Western Europe was the growing separation between parents and children there. In many regions in Western Europe, laws dictating that land and property be passed down to one's children did not exist. This weakened ties between parents and children, so children west of the Hajnal Line became free to make their own way in the world rather than being tied to the land generation after generation. Some economists credit these weaker familial ties with the earlier rise of industrialization and capitalism in Western Europe compared to Eastern Europe. Since many in Western Europe were free to migrate elsewhere, they could pursue objectives other than farming. This resulted in some taking up occupations enabling them to invent new machines or to come up with new ideas, thereby helping Western Europe develop more quickly than the rest of the continent.

*Glossary

birthrate: the proportion of births to the total population of a place

mortality rate: the proportion of deaths to the total population of a place

1 The author discusses "Hungarian economist John Hajnal" in paragraph 1 in order to

Ⓐ name the title of the paper that he wrote focusing on the Hajnal Line

Ⓑ argue that he was not the first person to describe the Hajnal Line

Ⓒ show his thoughts on marriage rates and birthrates in Eastern Europe

Ⓓ describe his work on a sociological issue affecting some parts of Europe

Paragraph 1 is marked with an arrow (➡).

The Hajnal Line

➡ There are myriad differences between Western and Eastern Europe, including obvious ones related to language, culture, and history. One that may not be apparent at first glance is related to marriage and birthrates. In 1965, Hungarian economist John Hajnal published a paper claiming Europe could be divided into two distinct regions. The article proposed that an imaginary line, now called the Hajnal Line, running from Saint Petersburg, Russia, to Trieste, Italy, separated two highly different regions of Europe based upon marriage and birth statistics. The primary thrust of Hajnal's report was that in Western Europe, people married later in age and had fewer children than people in Eastern Europe did. It also pointed out there were weaker family ties between parents and children in Western Europe than in Eastern Europe.

*Glossary

birthrate: the proportion of births to the total population of a place

2   The word "taboo" in the passage is closest in meaning to

Ⓐ regulation

Ⓑ suspension

Ⓒ prohibition

Ⓓ participation

3   In paragraph 2, all of the following questions are answered EXCEPT:

Ⓐ When were people who were living in Eastern Europe the most likely to get married?

Ⓑ What sometimes caused people in Western Europe to get remarried?

Ⓒ What was the historical age of both men and women living in Western Europe to get married?

Ⓓ How did the marriage rates of people living in Roman times differ from those in modern times?

Paragraph 2 is marked with an arrow (➡).

4   In paragraph 2, the author implies that Western European women

Ⓐ did not give birth to as many children as they were physically capable of doing

Ⓑ often had birth out of wedlock and then raised their children by themselves

Ⓒ preferred to get married at a younger age than most Eastern European women did

Ⓓ had a relatively high birthrate that resulted in a population increase in Western Europe

Paragraph 2 is marked with an arrow (➡).

➡ Throughout European history, the age of marriage has varied greatly. But as far back as Roman times, historical records show that men and women in Western Europe typically got married in their early twenties as opposed to people in Eastern European regions, where they more commonly married in their late teens. In Western Europe, the historic average age of marriage for women was twenty-four, and it was twenty-six for men. Roughly ten percent of the population never married, and, in some cases, such as after being widowed or divorced, people married a second time. Hajnal also detected a considerable lag between the time women were capable of having children and actually giving birth. The average age when most women are able to give birth is fourteen. With Western European women getting married at the average age of twenty-four, many of their childbearing years went unutilized. Coupled with some people never marrying and a strict taboo on birth out of wedlock, the result was a lower birthrate in comparison to Eastern Europe.

5 According to paragraph 3, which of the following is true about the Hajnal Line?

- Ⓐ There are places in Western Europe that do not follow the patterns which it predicts.
- Ⓑ It can be extended to places in Ireland, Finland, Spain, and Italy.
- Ⓒ Its existence takes into account various catastrophes, such as the Irish Potato Famine.
- Ⓓ Marriage rates and birthrates west of it are always higher than those east of it.

Paragraph 3 is marked with an arrow (➡).

6 Which of the sentences below best expresses the essential information in the highlighted sentence in the passage? Incorrect answer choices change the meaning in important ways or leave out essential information.

With a better quality of life compared to those living in Eastern Europe, Western European families normally had better medical care and access to steady food supplies.

- Ⓐ Those individuals living in Eastern Europe did not always have access to the good hospitals that those in Western Europe had.
- Ⓑ The quality of life in Western Europe was better than in Eastern Europe thanks to abundant food and health care.
- Ⓒ People living in Western Europe typically had good lives because they were able to eat plenty of food and had good medical care.
- Ⓓ There was much more food in Western Europe, which allowed Western Europeans to have lives that were high in quality.

➡ Not every place west of the Hajnal Line fits that pattern though. Ireland, Finland, and parts of southern Italy and southern Spain have seen historically higher marriage rates, earlier marriages, and higher birthrates than other regions in Western Europe. Nevertheless, these were not consistent. For instance, birthrates in these regions fluctuated according to economic conditions. In Ireland, after the Irish Potato Famine in the late 1840s, birthrates declined considerably for several years as people married later and had fewer children because they feared the consequences if famine returned.

Economic stability also played a contributing role in the lower marriage rates and birthrates in most of Western Europe. With a better quality of life compared to those living in Eastern Europe, Western European families normally had better medical care and access to steady food supplies. This resulted in lower overall death rates and child mortality rates. Therefore, there was less emphasis on getting married early and having large families. Meanwhile, in Eastern Europe, where periodic waves of disease, famine, and war took their toll on human life, people felt a stronger urge to marry early, to start having children, and to have enough children to replace those who frequently lost their lives during childbirth or in their infancy.

*Glossary

mortality rate: the proportion of deaths to the total population of a place

7 The word "ostracized" in the passage is closest in meaning to

Ⓐ executed

Ⓑ imprisoned

Ⓒ repealed

Ⓓ banished

8 According to paragraph 6, Western Europe turned to capitalism before Eastern Europe because

Ⓐ fewer people in the west were tied to the land, so they did not have to lead farming lives

Ⓑ political leaders in Western Europe urged people to improve their countries' economies

Ⓒ people in the west were generally more creative and innovative than those in the east

Ⓓ there was more arable land in the west, so farmers were able to sell surplus food for money

Paragraph 6 is marked with an arrow (➡).

Religious reasons for the differences in marriage rates and birthrates have been proven to have had little bearing on the matter. Virtually all of Europe was Christian in one form or another for the last few centuries. While Christianity advocates marriage and starting families, it is not an obligation, nor are those who fail to do so ostracized from society.

➡ One additional factor affecting Western Europe was the growing separation between parents and children there. In many regions in Western Europe, laws dictating that land and property be passed down to one's children did not exist. This weakened ties between parents and children, so children west of the Hajnal Line became free to make their own way in the world rather than being tied to the land generation after generation. Some economists credit these weaker familial ties with the earlier rise of industrialization and capitalism in Western Europe compared to Eastern Europe. Since many in Western Europe were free to migrate elsewhere, they could pursue objectives other than farming. This resulted in some taking up occupations enabling them to invent new machines or to come up with new ideas, thereby helping Western Europe develop more quickly than the rest of the continent.

9   Look at the four squares [■] that indicate
    where the following sentence could be added
    to the passage.

    **This enabled some wealthy individuals to
    bequeath their possessions to the Church
    or other organizations when they died.**

    Where would the sentence best fit?

    Click on a square [■] to add the sentence to the passage.

One additional factor affecting Western Europe was the growing separation between parents and children there. In many regions in Western Europe, laws dictating that land and property be passed down to one's children did not exist. **1** This weakened ties between parents and children, so children west of the Hajnal Line became free to make their own way in the world rather than being tied to the land generation after generation. **2** Some economists credit these weaker familial ties with the earlier rise of industrialization and capitalism in Western Europe compared to Eastern Europe. **3** Since many in Western Europe were free to migrate elsewhere, they could pursue objectives other than farming. **4** This resulted in some taking up occupations enabling them to invent new machines or to come up with new ideas, thereby helping Western Europe develop more quickly than the rest of the continent.

10 **Directions:** An introductory sentence for a brief summary of the passage is provided below. Complete the summary by selecting the THREE answer choices that express the most important ideas of the passage. Some sentences do not belong because they express ideas that are not presented in the passage or are minor ideas in the passage. **This question is worth 2 points.**

> Drag your answer choices to the spaces where they belong. To remove an answer choice, click on it. To review the passage, click on **VIEW TEXT.**

The Hajnal Line divides Eastern and Western Europe according to both birthrates and marriage rates.

-
-
-

ANSWER CHOICES

1. Many people in Western Europe were not tied to their land, but that was not the case of people in Eastern Europe.

2. Because there was more economic stability in the western part of Europe than in the east, people in the west tended to have children later in life.

3. Throughout history, individuals who live in Eastern Europe have traditionally gotten married earlier than those living in Western Europe did.

4. There were some religious differences between people living in the east and west, but most people in Europe in the past were Christian.

5. According to John Hajnal, the Hajnal Line starts in the city of St. Petersburg, Russia, and goes all the way to the Italian city of Trieste.

6. Parents and children in Western Europe were often separated since people were not tied to the land, and that resulted in industrialization and capitalism developing there.

Chemical Weathering

Weathering is a natural process through which rocks are broken down into smaller pieces in various manners. One of the main ways this occurs is through chemical changes in rocks, which cause them to break apart. For chemical weathering to happen, there must be a source of water—typically rainwater— present. It normally takes place on exposed rock unprotected by vegetation. Weathering is additionally more common in humid climates with heavy rainfall. It is also possible for humans to cause chemical weathering through the pumping of various substances into the atmosphere, which produce acid rain. There are three major types of chemical weathering: carbonation, hydrolysis, and oxidation.

Carbonation weathering results from rock being subjected to the exposure of rainwater that is acidic in composition. Carbon dioxide in the atmosphere can dissolve in rainwater, which subsequently produces a form of acid that can be weak or strong, depending upon the composition of the atmosphere. In areas with a large amount of pollution or soon after a volcanic eruption, high levels of sulfuric acid in the air can produce strong sulfuric acid rainwater. When acidic rainwater strikes rocks, it seeps into cracks. The acidic water affects certain minerals by causing them to break apart from the main rock formation. Especially vulnerable are rocks made of calcium carbonate. The most common rock formation that carbonation affects is limestone. In exposed limestone formations, small cracks initially expand and create larger ones, giving the limestone an appearance like cracked pavement. As the acidic water dissolves more rock, it may drip deep underground and create limestone formations such as <u>stalagmites</u> and <u>stalactites</u> in caves. Other rocks, including chalk and halite, can be affected by carbonation while some rocks, such as quartz, are stronger and dissolve at slower rates.

Hydrolysis weathering is caused by a chemical reaction between water and rock, particularly those rocks containing silicates. Through an exchange of atoms between the water and the rock's mineral composition, a transformation takes place. The most common example of this is feldspar, a mineral found

in granite formations. As water comes into contact with granite, the feldspar crystals undergo a change, becoming clay. This transformation weakens the granite, so it begins to break apart. Over a long enough period of time, weathered feldspar can leave behind enormous deposits of clay. This clay is normally white and is called kaolin, which is valuable for making porcelain ceramics. Hydrolysis additionally sometimes affects statues and buildings comprised of a high percentage of granite by causing them to have a pitted appearance in places where the feldspar in them has transformed into clay.

Oxidation weathering is the result of a reaction in minerals in rocks upon being exposed to oxygen. The most common form of oxidation weathering is the reaction of iron when combined with oxygen and water. It forms iron oxide, also known as rust, when oxygen atoms attract electrons from iron atoms, thereby weakening the rock, which results in it breaking apart. Sodium and magnesium are two more elements which can be easily oxidized. The oxygen may come directly from the atmosphere or from a source of water falling on rocks. Oxidation is easily recognized by its reddish hue in rock formations where it occurs. Ayers Rock in Australia is a large monolith-like rock that rises out of a flat plain. Its distinctive red appearance is the result of the oxidation of the iron-bearing rock on its outer surface.

Chemical weathering is not an overnight process but can take thousands—or even millions—of years before it affects exposed rock formations. In addition, depending upon the composition, more than one type of chemical weathering can occur in the same rock formation. The process of chemical weathering also creates numerous unique rock formations. One of the major indications of chemical weathering is rocks that appear pitted. Other weathered rocks appear like spheres; some are small while others are very large. Spheres form in rock formations with large cracks called joints. These grow larger as the rock is pushed up out of the ground. The various chemical weathering processes can expand these joints by initially forming rounded edges and then by breaking rock away from the larger formation. The result is a field of sphere-shaped rocks.

*Glossary

stalagmite: a deposit often made of calcium carbonate that forms on the floor of cave due to the extensive dripping of water

stalactite: a deposit often made of calcium carbonate that forms on the ceiling of a cave and has an icicle-like appearance due to the extensive dripping of water

PASSAGE 2

REVIEW

HELP

BACK

NEXT

HIDE TIME 00:54:00

Beginning

11 According to paragraph 1, which of the following is NOT true about weathering?

Ⓐ The results of some natural processes send chemicals into the air, which create acid rain.

Ⓑ It tends to take place more often in geographical areas that receive large amounts of precipitation.

Ⓒ Without the presence of water in some form, there is no way for it to be able to take place.

Ⓓ There are several natural ways that it is able to work to break down rocks in certain areas.

Paragraph 1 is marked with an arrow (➡).

Chemical Weathering

➡ Weathering is a natural process through which rocks are broken down into smaller pieces in various manners. One of the main ways this occurs is through chemical changes in rocks, which cause them to break apart. For chemical weathering to happen, there must be a source of water— typically rainwater—present. It normally takes place on exposed rock unprotected by vegetation. Weathering is additionally more common in humid climates with heavy rainfall. It is also possible for humans to cause chemical weathering through the pumping of various substances into the atmosphere, which produce acid rain. There are three major types of chemical weathering: carbonation, hydrolysis, and oxidation.

12 The phrase "seeps into" in the passage is closest in meaning to

- (A) speeds into
- (B) resides in
- (C) trickles into
- (D) moves away from

13 In paragraph 2, why does the author mention "cracked pavement"?

- (A) To prove that weathering is strong enough to affect concrete
- (B) To explain how artificial structures can be weathered at times
- (C) To show one of the possible effects of carbonation weathering
- (D) To point out how easily rocks such as limestone can be weathered

Paragraph 2 is marked with an arrow (➡).

➡ Carbonation weathering results from rock being subjected to the exposure of rainwater that is acidic in composition. Carbon dioxide in the atmosphere can dissolve in rainwater, which subsequently produces a form of acid that can be weak or strong, depending upon the composition of the atmosphere. In areas with a large amount of pollution or soon after a volcanic eruption, high levels of sulfuric acid in the air can produce strong sulfuric acid rainwater. When acidic rainwater strikes rocks, it seeps into cracks. The acidic water affects certain minerals by causing them to break apart from the main rock formation. Especially vulnerable are rocks made of calcium carbonate. The most common rock formation that carbonation affects is limestone. In exposed limestone formations, small cracks initially expand and create larger ones, giving the limestone an appearance like cracked pavement. As the acidic water dissolves more rock, it may drip deep underground and create limestone formations such as stalagmites and stalactites in caves. Other rocks, including chalk and halite, can be affected by carbonation while some rocks, such as quartz, are stronger and dissolve at slower rates.

*Glossary

stalagmite: a deposit often made of calcium carbonate that forms on the floor of cave due to the extensive dripping of water

stalactite: a deposit often made of calcium carbonate that forms on the ceiling of a cave and has an icicle-like appearance due to the extensive dripping of water

14 Which of the sentences below best expresses the essential information in the highlighted sentence in the passage? Incorrect answer choices change the meaning in important ways or leave out essential information.

Hydrolysis additionally sometimes affects statues and buildings comprised of a high percentage of granite by causing them to have a pitted appearance in places where the feldspar in them has transformed into clay.

Ⓐ Buildings and other structures made primarily of granite can be affected by hydrolysis when parts of them turn into clay, which makes them look pitted.

Ⓑ People have begun to make buildings and statues from granite because ones that they make with feldspar can turn into clay and begin to look pitted.

Ⓒ It is possible to make buildings and sculptures with granite, but through the process of hydrolysis, they can be transformed into clay at times.

Ⓓ When the process of hydrolysis affects feldspar, it is capable of turning the feldspar found in granite into a substance similar to clay.

15 According to paragraph 3, kaolin may be created because

Ⓐ the feldspar found in granite works together with water to transform other minerals into it

Ⓑ the presence of granite in large amounts can help produce weathering effects in feldspar

Ⓒ hydrolysis weathering affects minerals that are found in granite and changes them into clay

Ⓓ exposure to oxygen and water makes the feldspar located in granite transform over time

Paragraph 3 is marked with an arrow (➡).

➡ Hydrolysis weathering is caused by a chemical reaction between water and rock, particularly those rocks containing silicates. Through an exchange of atoms between the water and the rock's mineral composition, a transformation takes place. The most common example of this is feldspar, a mineral found in granite formations. As water comes into contact with granite, the feldspar crystals undergo a change, becoming clay. This transformation weakens the granite, so it begins to break apart. Over a long enough period of time, weathered feldspar can leave behind enormous deposits of clay. This clay is normally white and is called kaolin, which is valuable for making porcelain ceramics. Hydrolysis additionally sometimes affects statues and buildings comprised of a high percentage of granite by causing them to have a pitted appearance in places where the feldspar in them has transformed into clay.

16 What is the author's purpose in paragraph 4 of the passage?

(A) To explain why oxidation only affects certain types of rocks while leaving others alone

(B) To stress some of the negative effects of the rust that is created by chemical weathering

(C) To name one of the best-known places in the world that was affected by oxidation

(D) To describe both the causes and the effects of one type of natural chemical weathering

Paragraph 4 is marked with an arrow (➡).

17 According to paragraph 4, which of the following is true about oxidation?

(A) It is capable not only of breaking apart rocks but also of altering their coloring.

(B) It takes the longest of all the types of chemical weathering to break down rocks.

(C) It is able to turn any rocks that it affects into rust over a short period of time.

(D) It cannot take place unless elements such as sodium and magnesium are present.

Paragraph 4 is marked with an arrow (➡).

18 In paragraph 5, the author implies that rock formations

(A) can only be affected by a single type of chemical weathering at one time

(B) have been known to be shaped by chemical weathering in a matter of hours or days

(C) are almost always turned into spherical shapes whenever chemical weathering affects them

(D) can assume a variety of different shapes due to the effects of chemical weathering

Paragraph 5 is marked with an arrow (⇨).

➡ Oxidation weathering is the result of a reaction in minerals in rocks upon being exposed to oxygen. The most common form of oxidation weathering is the reaction of iron when combined with oxygen and water. It forms iron oxide, also known as rust, when oxygen atoms attract electrons from iron atoms, thereby weakening the rock, which results in it breaking apart. Sodium and magnesium are two more elements which can be easily oxidized. The oxygen may come directly from the atmosphere or from a source of water falling on rocks. Oxidation is easily recognized by its reddish hue in rock formations where it occurs. Ayers Rock in Australia is a large monolith-like rock that rises out of a flat plain. Its distinctive red appearance is the result of the oxidation of the iron-bearing rock on its outer surface.

⇨ Chemical weathering is not an overnight process but can take thousands—or even millions—of years before it affects exposed rock formations. In addition, depending upon the composition, more than one type of chemical weathering can occur in the same rock formation. The process of chemical weathering also creates numerous unique rock formations. One of the major indications of chemical weathering is rocks that appear pitted. Other weathered rocks appear like spheres; some are small while others are very large. Spheres form in rock formations with large cracks called joints. These grow larger as the rock is pushed up out of the ground. The various chemical weathering processes can expand these joints by initially forming rounded edges and then by breaking rock away from the larger formation. The result is a field of sphere-shaped rocks.

19 Look at the four squares [■] that indicate where the following sentence could be added to the passage.

In addition, buildings and other structures made of limestone can be weathered when enough rain that is acidic in nature falls on them.

Where would the sentence best fit?

Click on a square [■] to add the sentence to the passage.

Carbonation weathering results from rock being subjected to the exposure of rainwater that is acidic in composition. Carbon dioxide in the atmosphere can dissolve in rainwater, which subsequently produces a form of acid that can be weak or strong, depending upon the composition of the atmosphere. In areas with a large amount of pollution or soon after a volcanic eruption, high levels of sulfuric acid in the air can produce strong sulfuric acid rainwater. When acidic rainwater strikes rocks, it seeps into cracks. The acidic water affects certain minerals by causing them to break apart from the main rock formation. Especially vulnerable are rocks made of calcium carbonate. The most common rock formation that carbonation affects is limestone. **1** In exposed limestone formations, small cracks initially expand and create larger ones, giving the limestone an appearance like cracked pavement. **2** As the acidic water dissolves more rock, it may drip deep underground and create limestone formations such as stalagmites and stalactites in caves. **3** Other rocks, including chalk and halite, can be affected by carbonation while some rocks, such as quartz, are stronger and dissolve at slower rates. **4**

*Glossary

stalagmite: a deposit often made of calcium carbonate that forms on the floor of cave due to the extensive dripping of water

stalactite: a deposit often made of calcium carbonate that forms on the ceiling of a cave and has an icicle-like appearance due to the extensive dripping of water

20 Directions: An introductory sentence for a brief summary of the passage is provided below. Complete the summary by selecting the THREE answer choices that express the most important ideas of the passage. Some sentences do not belong because they express ideas that are not presented in the passage or are minor ideas in the passage. **This question is worth 2 points.**

> Drag your answer choices to the spaces where they belong. To remove an answer choice, click on it. To review the passage, click on **VIEW TEXT**.

Chemical weathering is a process that can result in rocks being broken down in a variety of ways.

-
-
-

ANSWER CHOICES

1 Acid rain is one type of chemical weathering that is produced by humans and does not occur naturally.

2 Hydrolysis is one process which, thanks to the actions of water, can break down rocks and turn some of them into different substances.

3 Exposure to rainwater over a period of time can cause carbonation weathering to occur in soft rocks such as limestone.

4 Carbonation weathering can produce large gaps underground that then result in caves being formed.

5 It is possible for a combination of oxygen and water to break apart some rocks and even to change their colors.

6 Scientists believe that they know how to reverse the effects of some types of chemical weathering.

Saltwater and Freshwater Crabs

Japanese spider crab, a saltwater crab

Potamon ibericum, a freshwater crab

The crab is one of the most common shellfish as more than 4,500 species dwell in places around the globe. These creatures can be divided into two main types: saltwater crabs and freshwater crabs. Saltwater crabs comprise roughly two-thirds of the total number of crab species and are by far more familiar to people than their freshwater cousins. Despite possessing some similarities, these two types of crabs have a number of important differences.

The similarities are primarily of a superficial nature. For instance, both have bodies with similar shapes, being rounded or oval and covered with a hardened shell which periodically molts and grows back larger in size. They have ten jointed appendages with the two front ones, called pincers, most commonly being larger than the others, and they additionally have two eyes on <u>stalks</u> above their mouths. They reproduce by laying eggs the female carries until they hatch and are omnivorous, devouring virtually anything edible they come across as well. Finally, each type of crab plays a crucial role in filtering algae and other material from water, thereby ensuring cleaner water systems wherever they reside.

The differences, however, between the two crabs, are more prominent and show a distinct divide between the species. Most notable among them is their habitats. Saltwater crabs live in salty oceans near the shore or sometimes in deep regions whereas freshwater crabs can be found in rivers, deltas, estuaries, caves, swamps, and other inshore regions containing fresh water. All crabs have gills, permitting them to separate oxygen from water, and most additionally have the ability to breathe air on land. However, except for a few exclusively land-living freshwater crabs, they must return to water to survive at some point. Still, each can only survive in either a saltwater or freshwater environment. To dwell in oceans, saltwater crab gills evolved to lower the <u>salinity level</u> of water entering their gills. In addition, some saltwater species live in water as deep as 600 meters, so their bodies are capable of withstanding frigid temperatures and intense water pressure.

Some other variations concern where and how the crabs reside. Many freshwater crab species live as individuals or in relatively small groups while saltwater crab groups dwarf freshwater crabs in size. As an example, tens of thousands of red king crabs can be found at depths of two hundred meters dwelling in massive colonies in the waters off the American state of Alaska. Freshwater crabs are also more likely to seek shelter than saltwater crabs as they might live in crevices in rocky walls or caves while some burrow into sand, soft soil, or mud nearby water, forming tunnel-like structures. The chief purpose of sheltering is to hide themselves from predators during daylight hours. When the sun goes down, freshwater crabs emerge from their shelters and seek food. Another reason that females find shelter is to locate safe places to hatch their eggs. When that happens, the larvae can survive longer if they hatch in a shelter protected from predators.

Physically, saltwater crabs are larger than freshwater crabs. Many freshwater crabs are small enough to fit in a person's hand, but some species of saltwater crabs, such as Japanese spider crabs, have a stretched-out span greater than the height of an average human. Some have been measured with a span of more than four meters. Freshwater crabs normally lay fewer eggs than saltwater crabs. After mating, they may lay a few hundred eggs at once, but saltwater crabs are capable of laying thousands. This has led to a greater propagation of saltwater crabs whereas the lack of large numbers of offspring has caused many freshwater species to be in danger of extinction.

Yet another danger faced by freshwater crabs concerns their habitats, which tend to be shallow waters located near places where animals and humans reside. Not only marine predators but also numerous birds and land predators hunt freshwater crabs and make them part of their diets. On the other hand, saltwater crabs frequently dwell in deep ocean regions and therefore have fewer predators other than humans. Indeed, it is commercial fishermen who account for most of their losses each year as they harvest nearly one and a half million tons of crabs from the world's oceans annually.

*Glossary

stalk: a slender supporting structure on an animal upon which a body part, such as an eye, may be attached

salinity level: the amount of salt in a substance, particularly a liquid

21 Which of the sentences below best expresses the essential information in the highlighted sentence in the passage? Incorrect answer choices change the meaning in important ways or leave out essential information.

Saltwater crabs comprise roughly two-thirds of the total number of crab species and are by far more familiar to people than their freshwater cousins.

- (A) While there are two times more saltwater crabs than freshwater ones, the latter are much better known.
- (B) Freshwater crabs are not familiar to people because there are simply not many of them in existence.
- (C) More people know about the more numerous saltwater crabs than are aware of freshwater ones.
- (D) There are thousands of species of saltwater crabs, making them the best-known shellfish in the world.

22 The word "superficial" in the passage is closest in meaning to

- (A) apparent
- (B) physical
- (C) minor
- (D) subtle

Saltwater and Freshwater Crabs

The crab is one of the most common shellfish as more than 4,500 species dwell in places around the globe. These creatures can be divided into two main types: saltwater crabs and freshwater crabs. Saltwater crabs comprise roughly two-thirds of the total number of crab species and are by far more familiar to people than their freshwater cousins. Despite possessing some similarities, these two types of crabs have a number of important differences.

The similarities are primarily of a superficial nature. For instance, both have bodies with similar shapes, being rounded or oval and covered with a hardened shell which periodically molts and grows back larger in size. They have ten jointed appendages with the two front ones, called pincers, most commonly being larger than the others, and they additionally have two eyes on stalks above their mouths. They reproduce by laying eggs the female carries until they hatch and are omnivorous, devouring virtually anything edible they come across as well. Finally, each type of crab plays a crucial role in filtering algae and other material from water, thereby ensuring cleaner water systems wherever they reside.

*Glossary

stalk: a slender supporting structure on an animal upon which a body part, such as an eye, may be attached

More Available

23 According to paragraph 3, saltwater crabs are able to live in the ocean because

(A) they need to hide from the numerous predators living there

(B) their bodies can handle the large amounts of salt that are found in the water

(C) they do not live so deep that they are affected by the water pressure

(D) their hardened shells allow them to resist the high salinity level of the water

Paragraph 3 is marked with an arrow (➡).

24 In paragraph 3, which of the following can be inferred about saltwater crabs?

(A) Water pressure harms them more than it affects freshwater crabs.

(B) Cold weather does not have a negative effect on some of them.

(C) Some of them lay their eggs in swamps and estuaries.

(D) A few of them are capable of living out of the water permanently.

Paragraph 3 is marked with an arrow (➡).

➡ The differences, however, between the two crabs, are more prominent and show a distinct divide between the species. Most notable among them is their habitats. Saltwater crabs live in salty oceans near the shore or sometimes in deep regions whereas freshwater crabs can be found in rivers, deltas, estuaries, caves, swamps, and other inshore regions containing fresh water. All crabs have gills, permitting them to separate oxygen from water, and most additionally have the ability to breathe air on land. However, except for a few exclusively land-living freshwater crabs, they must return to water to survive at some point. Still, each can only survive in either a saltwater or freshwater environment. To dwell in oceans, saltwater crab gills evolved to lower the salinity level of water entering their gills. In addition, some saltwater species live in water as deep as 600 meters, so their bodies are capable of withstanding frigid temperatures and intense water pressure.

*Glossary

salinity level: the amount of salt in a substance, particularly a liquid

25 In stating that saltwater crab groups "dwarf freshwater crabs in size," the author means that saltwater crab groups

  (A) resemble freshwater crab groups

  (B) attack freshwater crab groups

  (C) outnumber freshwater crab groups

  (D) avoid freshwater crab groups

26 In paragraph 4, all of the following questions are answered EXCEPT:

  (A) What part of the day do freshwater crabs become active and then hunt for food?

  (B) Why do freshwater crabs tend to live as individuals rather than in large colonies?

  (C) What is the primary reason that freshwater crabs search for places to hide?

  (D) How large are some of the colonies of red king crabs that live off the Alaskan coast?

Paragraph 4 is marked with an arrow (➡).

➡ Some other variations concern where and how the crabs reside. Many freshwater crab species live as individuals or in relatively small groups while saltwater crab groups dwarf freshwater crabs in size. As an example, tens of thousands of red king crabs can be found at depths of two hundred meters dwelling in massive colonies in the waters off the American state of Alaska. Freshwater crabs are also more likely to seek shelter than saltwater crabs as they might live in crevices in rocky walls or caves while some burrow into sand, soft soil, or mud nearby water, forming tunnel-like structures. The chief purpose of sheltering is to hide themselves from predators during daylight hours. When the sun goes down, freshwater crabs emerge from their shelters and seek food. Another reason that females find shelter is to locate safe places to hatch their eggs. When that happens, the larvae can survive longer if they hatch in a shelter protected from predators.

27 The author discusses "Japanese spider crabs" in paragraph 5 in order to

(A) explain the reason that the species is in serious danger of going extinct

(B) emphasize their large size in comparison with that of freshwater crabs

(C) point out the amount of meat that can be harvested from a single crab

(D) mention how many eggs females of the species have been known to lay

Paragraph 5 is marked with an (➡).

28 According to paragraph 6, which of the following is true about freshwater crabs?

(A) Humans are primarily responsible for the reduction in their numbers worldwide.

(B) More than one million tons of them are hunted by fishermen to use as food sources.

(C) There are animals residing both on land and in the water that hunt them for food.

(D) They have fewer predators than saltwater crabs on account of where their habitats are.

Paragraph 6 is marked with an arrow (⇨).

➡ Physically, saltwater crabs are larger than freshwater crabs. Many freshwater crabs are small enough to fit in a person's hand, but some species of saltwater crabs, such as Japanese spider crabs, have a stretched-out span greater than the height of an average human. Some have been measured with a span of more than four meters. Freshwater crabs normally lay fewer eggs than saltwater crabs. After mating, they may lay a few hundred eggs at once, but saltwater crabs are capable of laying thousands. This has led to a greater propagation of saltwater crabs whereas the lack of large numbers of offspring has caused many freshwater species to be in danger of extinction.

⇨ Yet another danger faced by freshwater crabs concerns their habitats, which tend to be shallow waters located near places where animals and humans reside. Not only marine predators but also numerous birds and land predators hunt freshwater crabs and make them part of their diets. On the other hand, saltwater crabs frequently dwell in deep ocean regions and therefore have fewer predators other than humans. Indeed, it is commercial fishermen who account for most of their losses each year as they harvest nearly one and a half million tons of crabs from the world's oceans annually.

29 Look at the four squares [■] that indicate where the following sentence could be added to the passage.

They are also prone to being devoured by predators, which means that a fairly small percentage of them ever hatch.

Where would the sentence best fit?

Click on a square [■] to add the sentence to the passage.

Physically, saltwater crabs are larger than freshwater crabs. **1** Many freshwater crabs are small enough to fit in a person's hand, but some species of saltwater crabs, such as Japanese spider crabs, have a stretched-out span greater than the height of an average human. **2** Some have been measured with a span of more than four meters. **3** Freshwater crabs normally lay fewer eggs than saltwater crabs. **4** After mating, they may lay a few hundred eggs at once, but saltwater crabs are capable of laying thousands. This has led to a greater propagation of saltwater crabs whereas the lack of large numbers of offspring has caused many freshwater species to be in danger of extinction.

30 Directions: Select the appropriate statements from the answer choices and match them to the type of crab to which they relate. TWO of the answer choices will NOT be used. **This question is worth 3 points.**

> Drag your answer choices to the spaces where they belong. To remove an answer choice, click on it. To review the passage, click on **VIEW TEXT**.

ANSWER CHOICES

1. Is the object of restoration efforts by humans to increase its numbers

2. May lay thousands of eggs at a single time

3. Is known to live in water that is shallow as well as in very deep places

4. Tends to make its home near those of humans and other predators

5. Is found living in or around all of the continents on the Earth

6. Often digs into the soil in order to hide itself

7. Is the more numerous type of crab with regard to species

TYPE OF CRAB

Saltwater (Select 3)

- •
- •
- •

Freshwater (Select 2)

- •
- •

Actual Test

09

Reading Section Directions

This section measures your ability to understand academic passages in English. You will have **54 minutes** to read and answer questions about **3 passages**. A clock at the top of the screen will show you how much time is remaining.

Most questions are worth 1 point but the last question for each passage is worth more than 1 point. The directions for the last question indicate how many points you may receive.

Some passages include a word or phrase that is underlined. Click on the word or phrase to see a definition or an explanation.

When you want to move to the next question, click on **NEXT**. You may skip questions and go back to them later. If you want to return to previous questions, click on **BACK**. You can click on **REVIEW** at any time, and the review screen will show you which questions you have answered and which you have not answered. From this review screen, you may go directly to any question you have already seen in the Reading section.

Click on **CONTINUE** to go on.

Diapause in Insects

a butterfly pupa

Diapause refers to the period of <u>dormancy</u> in the lifecycle of an insect. This state may be a part of its natural lifecycle or a reaction to some sort of environmental stimulus, such as a change in the length of a day, a change in temperature, or a lack of available food. The main purpose of diapause is to protect the insect while it is developing or to enable it to survive adverse environmental conditions. Diapause can occur at any stage of an insect's lifecycle, from the egg stage to the adult stage, and it typically begins with a genetic stimulus that triggers the insect to initiate preparations for dormancy. This is followed by the dormancy stage, which concludes when another stimulus prompts the insect to become active again.

There are two primary types of insect diapause: obligatory and facultative. The former occurs no matter what type of environmental conditions exist as it is a natural part of an insect's lifecycle, so it may occur during relatively benign conditions or during less ideal ones. A common example of obligatory diapause is the pupae stage many insects enter prior to becoming adults. In contrast, facultative diapause happens only in response to changes in an insect's environment. Insects which undergo obligatory diapause normally produce only a single generation annually whereas those that undergo facultative diapause may create two or more generations each year. Because these generations are spread out over the course of a year, some generations encounter severe environmental conditions, particularly changes in temperature, which force them to become dormant. A third—rarer—type of diapause is reproduction diapause, in which mating is temporarily suspended. The monarch butterfly practices this in late summer and early autumn as it conserves energy for its long migratory flight from northern regions to Mexico.

Some common characteristics of the two main types of diapause are the slowing of physical development, a reduction in metabolism, a lack of mating and reproduction, and an increase in protection against outside stressors. Biologists believe all of these factors are triggered at the genetic level. Genetic

triggers reduce mating, for instance, by shutting down the drive to reproduce in males, females, or both, as is the case with monarch butterflies. In some cases, such as with wasps, mating occurs before the insects enter diapause so that females may later produce eggs even if many males fail to survive the diapause stage. Other genetic triggers are activated by changes in the environment. In northern regions, as winter approaches, these changes include the shortening of daylight hours and cooling weather. In deserts and tropical regions, seasonal changes altering the availability of food sources can also trigger diapause.

Once an insect's genes initiate diapause, it begins preparing to enter dormancy. It gathers and stores food in its body to utilize during that time and later after it reawakens. The insect must take in enough nutrients to survive the dormancy and reawakening periods until it can be revived sufficiently to begin searching for food. The length of the diapause period varies from species to species and often depends on the length of the adverse conditions. For some insects, it lasts only a few months, but it can be more than a year for others. Normally, in temperate zones, diapause lasts up to nine months. Extended diapause lasting more than a year has been witnessed in more than sixty insect species. One such instance is the wheat blossom midge, which can remain dormant in the soil in its larval stage for up to three years.

There are several inherent dangers for insects entering diapause, among them being a fluctuation in environmental conditions that prompts them to emerge from dormancy too soon. A warm spring followed by a late frost may kill countless insects that reawaken too soon. There is also the possibility of not taking in enough nutrients to sufficiently feed itself even at low metabolic rates. Finally, while dormant, unless it is well hidden, the insect is vulnerable to predators and is additionally unable to defend itself or flee from danger. Despite these facts, most insect species exist in sufficient numbers to ensure that enough survive each period of diapause to produce the ensuing generation.

*Glossary

dormancy: the state of being at rest or inactive

frost: a condition in which the weather is cold enough to make water freeze

Beginning ▲

Diapause in Insects

➡ Diapause refers to the period of <u>dormancy</u> in the lifecycle of an insect. This state may be a part of its natural lifecycle or a reaction to some sort of environmental stimulus, such as a change in the length of a day, a change in temperature, or a lack of available food. The main purpose of diapause is to protect the insect while it is developing or to enable it to survive adverse environmental conditions. Diapause can occur at any stage of an insect's lifecycle, from the egg stage to the adult stage, and it typically begins with a genetic stimulus that triggers the insect to initiate preparations for dormancy. This is followed by the dormancy stage, which concludes when another stimulus prompts the insect to become active again.

1 The word "adverse" in the passage is closest in meaning to

   Ⓐ unusual

   Ⓑ extensive

   Ⓒ hostile

   Ⓓ cold

Paragraph 1 is marked with an arrow (➡).

2 According to paragraph 1, insects may go through diapause because

   Ⓐ they are returning from long migrations and need to rest their bodies

   Ⓑ they are preparing to enter the reproductive stage in their lives

   Ⓒ they are affected in some way by a change in their environment

   Ⓓ they are reacting to the actions of the predators living near them

Paragraph 1 is marked with an arrow (➡).

*Glossary

dormancy: the state of being at rest or inactive

3 In paragraph 2, the author's description of facultative diapause mentions all of the following EXCEPT:

- (A) How the environment can affect insects that endure it
- (B) The name of an insect that is known to go through it
- (C) The reason why it may happen to insects
- (D) How frequently insects going through it reproduce

Paragraph 2 is marked with an arrow (➡).

4 In paragraph 2, the author uses "The monarch butterfly" as an example of

- (A) a butterfly which spends a lot of its life in parts of Mexico
- (B) one of the few insects that is known to engage in migratory behavior
- (C) the best-known example of an insect that may become dormant
- (D) an insect that goes through a type of diapause which is less common

Paragraph 2 is marked with an arrow (➡).

➡ There are two primary types of insect diapause: obligatory and facultative. The former occurs no matter what type of environmental conditions exist as it is a natural part of an insect's lifecycle, so it may occur during relatively benign conditions or during less ideal ones. A common example of obligatory diapause is the pupae stage many insects enter prior to becoming adults. In contrast, facultative diapause happens only in response to changes in an insect's environment. Insects which undergo obligatory diapause normally produce only a single generation annually whereas those that undergo facultative diapause may create two or more generations each year. Because these generations are spread out over the course of a year, some generations encounter severe environmental conditions, particularly changes in temperature, which force them to become dormant. A third—rarer—type of diapause is reproduction diapause, in which mating is temporarily suspended. The monarch butterfly practices this in late summer and early autumn as it conserves energy for its long migratory flight from northern regions to Mexico.

5 In paragraph 3, which of the following can be inferred about diapause?

  (A) All insects mate prior to undergoing diapause to make sure the next generation survives.

  (B) Insects that go through diapause may experience a number of different changes.

  (C) Diapause lasts approximately the same amount of time for all insects.

  (D) Wasps and butterflies are the insects that most commonly go through diapause.

Paragraph 3 is marked with an arrow (➡).

6 The word "witnessed" in the passage is closest in meaning to

  (A) observed

  (B) considered

  (C) determined

  (D) repeated

7 According to paragraph 4, which of the following is true about diapause in insects?

  (A) Some insects awaken from dormancy, obtain food, and then go dormant again.

  (B) Insects are able to take nutrients into their bodies while they are going through diapause.

  (C) It is vital for insects to have a supply of food while they are in a dormant state.

  (D) Those insects living in temperate conditions tend to be dormant for only a few weeks.

Paragraph 4 is marked with an arrow (⇨).

➡ Some common characteristics of the two main types of diapause are the slowing of physical development, a reduction in metabolism, a lack of mating and reproduction, and an increase in protection against outside stressors. Biologists believe all of these factors are triggered at the genetic level. Genetic triggers reduce mating, for instance, by shutting down the drive to reproduce in males, females, or both, as is the case with monarch butterflies. In some cases, such as with wasps, mating occurs before the insects enter diapause so that females may later produce eggs even if many males fail to survive the diapause stage. Other genetic triggers are activated by changes in the environment. In northern regions, as winter approaches, these changes include the shortening of daylight hours and cooling weather. In deserts and tropical regions, seasonal changes altering the availability of food sources can also trigger diapause.

⇨ Once an insect's genes initiate diapause, it begins preparing to enter dormancy. It gathers and stores food in its body to utilize during that time and later after it reawakens. The insect must take in enough nutrients to survive the dormancy and reawakening periods until it can be revived sufficiently to begin searching for food. The length of the diapause period varies from species to species and often depends on the length of the adverse conditions. For some insects, it lasts only a few months, but it can be more than a year for others. Normally, in temperate zones, diapause lasts up to nine months. Extended diapause lasting more than a year has been witnessed in more than sixty insect species. One such instance is the wheat blossom midge, which can remain dormant in the soil in its larval stage for up to three years.

8 According to paragraph 5, which of the following is NOT true about the dangers of diapause?

Ⓐ Insects that do not get sufficient amounts of food may not be able to feed themselves.

Ⓑ Predators are able to find insects that are dormant and not well hidden.

Ⓒ Some insects emerge from it too quickly and then wind up dying as a result.

Ⓓ The eggs that are laid by insects going through diapause rarely hatch.

Paragraph 5 is marked with an arrow (➡).

➡ There are several inherent dangers for insects entering diapause, among them being a fluctuation in environmental conditions that prompts them to emerge from dormancy too soon. A warm spring followed by a late frost may kill countless insects that reawaken too soon. There is also the possibility of not taking in enough nutrients to sufficiently feed itself even at low metabolic rates. Finally, while dormant, unless it is well hidden, the insect is vulnerable to predators and is additionally unable to defend itself or flee from danger. Despite these facts, most insect species exist in sufficient numbers to ensure that enough survive each period of diapause to produce the ensuing generation.

*Glossary

frost: a condition in which the weather is cold enough to make water freeze

9   Look at the four squares [■] that indicate
    where the following sentence could be added
    to the passage.

    **This makes it easy prey for any animal
    which happens to come across it while
    hunting for food.**

    Where would the sentence best fit?

    Click on a square [■] to add the sentence to the passage.

There are several inherent dangers for insects entering diapause, among them being a fluctuation in environmental conditions that prompts them to emerge from dormancy too soon. **1** A warm spring followed by a late frost may kill countless insects that reawaken too soon. **2** There is also the possibility of not taking in enough nutrients to sufficiently feed itself even at low metabolic rates. **3** Finally, while dormant, unless it is well hidden, the insect is vulnerable to predators and is additionally unable to defend itself or flee from danger. **4** Despite these facts, most insect species exist in sufficient numbers to ensure that enough survive each period of diapause to produce the ensuing generation.

*Glossary

frost: a condition in which the weather is cold enough to make water freeze

10 **Directions:** An introductory sentence for a brief summary of the passage is provided below. Complete the summary by selecting the THREE answer choices that express the most important ideas of the passage. Some sentences do not belong because they express ideas that are not presented in the passage or are minor ideas in the passage. **This question is worth 2 points.**

Drag your answer choices to the spaces where they belong. To remove an answer choice, click on it. To review the passage, click on **VIEW TEXT**.

Diapause is a state of dormancy in insects that they may go through for various reasons.

-

-

-

ANSWER CHOICES

1. Sudden changes in the local environment can prompt a large number of insects to become dormant.

2. Insects may go through diapause because it is a part of their lifecycle, so they go dormant at a certain period in their lives.

3. It can be dangerous for insects to enter diapause due to both a lack of food and the presence of predators.

4. Only a few insects go through diapause for more than half a year at a single time.

5. Scientists are still trying to figure out what causes diapause and what the main reasons insects go through it are.

6. Most insects feel a need at the genetic level to obtain food prior to undergoing the diapause process.

Coral Reef Ecosystems

Reefs comprised of coral rank among the most critical of the Earth's ocean ecosystems. Containing a diverse range of marine flora and fauna, they are home to approximately twenty-five percent of all known marine lifeforms. The reefs are made of coral, a marine species that forms colonies of coral polyps which bind together thanks to secretions of calcium carbonate. They create rocklike formations that, when combined in large numbers, establish extensive reefs in shallow waters. Over time, plant life begins growing in reefs, and then animal life makes its way to them.

For a coral reef ecosystem to thrive, there must be adequate amounts of sunlight in addition to warm temperatures, so most reefs are located in shallow waters in tropical or subtropical regions. For the most part, they cannot exist in water deeper than fifty meters or in places where the water temperature is below twenty degrees Celsius. Some reefs can reach gargantuan sizes. The world's largest is the Great Barrier Reef, which stretches approximately 2,600 kilometers, off Australia's eastern coast. Some coral reefs grow so much that they ascend above the ocean's surface, creating coral atolls that typically surround large lagoons. One example is the Maldive Islands, which consist of around 1,200 coral atolls in the Indian Ocean.

The food chain in a reef is similar to that of other ecosystems; plant life supports some species, which are consumed by predators that are in turn hunted by apex predators. Each lifeform in a coral reef ecosystem is dependent upon other lifeforms, creating a vast symbiotic relationship structure. The first and most important relationship involved in the formation of coral reefs is that between coral polyps and plankton called zooxanthellae, a form of single-cell algae. They create food by photosynthesis, which the coral absorbs. In return, the coral provides the zooxanthellae with nutrients they require. The extra food the coral gathers lets it grow quicker than normal, enabling enough fast-growing coral polyps to form a large reef over the course of many years. Despite the enhanced growth, the formation of a reef is

a relatively slow process with scientists estimating that the world's extant coral reefs took thousands of years to attain their current forms. The Great Barrier Reef started forming approximately 20,000 years ago, but it is something of an outlier because the majority of reefs are much younger.

Once a reef is established, it attracts other marine lifeforms. Oftentimes, large patches of seagrasses take root alongside the reef. This is typical of fringing coral reefs, which are located near shore. Between the shore and the reef, seagrasses grow in large colonies. The reef provides protection for the seagrasses by preventing them from being uprooted from the seabed by strong waves whereas the seagrasses provide a high level of nutrients which small plankton feed on. These small plankton are afterward consumed by small fish and shellfish. Other marine lifeforms, such as sponges, grow on the reefs themselves. Sponges play a vital role by filtering water, so they break down large nutrient particles into smaller ones the coral and other lifeforms can absorb. Crabs and shrimp reside among the coral, where they gather food from the flowing water. Some of these creatures protect the coral from predators such as the crown-of-thorns starfish, an animal that actually consumes coral and serves as a major threat to some reefs.

As a coral reef expands, its lifeforms diversify. Marine biologists estimate that more than 4,000 fish species live in or around reefs. Small fish are consumed by larger fish, which are subsequently eaten by larger predators, including sharks, sturgeons, and eels. All kinds of seabirds are attracted to the surfaces of reefs due to their abundant food sources. This tremendous amount of life then attracts the world's most dangerous predator: humans. The overfishing of coral reefs has become a major global issue. Humans often destroy delicately balanced coral reef ecosystems by removing certain lifeforms in great numbers. Pollution is another serious threat worldwide because it kills numerous species and promptly upsets the balance in reefs. In recent years, however, efforts to protect coral reefs from fishing and pollution, such as in the endangered Belize Barrier Reef in Central America, have shown promise.

*Glossary

calcium carbonate: a white crystal, often powdery substance found in nature in limestone, chalk, and the secretions of some animals

apex predator: an animal that is at the top of the food chain and has no natural enemies that hunt it

Coral Reef Ecosystems

➡ Reefs comprised of coral rank among the most critical of the Earth's ocean ecosystems. Containing a diverse range of marine flora and fauna, they are home to approximately twenty-five percent of all known marine lifeforms. The reefs are made of coral, a marine species that forms colonies of coral polyps which bind together thanks to secretions of calcium carbonate. They create rocklike formations that, when combined in large numbers, establish extensive reefs in shallow waters. Over time, plant life begins growing in reefs, and then animal life makes its way to them.

⇨ For a coral reef ecosystem to thrive, there must be adequate amounts of sunlight in addition to warm temperatures, so most reefs are located in shallow waters in tropical or subtropical regions. For the most part, they cannot exist in water deeper than fifty meters or in places where the water temperature is below twenty degrees Celsius. Some reefs can reach gargantuan sizes. The world's largest is the Great Barrier Reef, which stretches approximately 2,600 kilometers, off Australia's eastern coast. Some coral reefs grow so much that they ascend above the ocean's surface, creating coral atolls that typically surround large lagoons. One example is the Maldive Islands, which consist of around 1,200 coral atolls in the Indian Ocean.

11 According to paragraph 1, which of the following is NOT true about coral reefs?

Ⓐ Plants first start growing in them, and then animals are attracted to them later.

Ⓑ Roughly one quarter of all of the animals on the Earth can be found living in them.

Ⓒ They form when certain animals secrete a substance that makes reefs over time.

Ⓓ Many people consider them to be some of the most important ecosystems in oceans.

Paragraph 1 is marked with an arrow (➡).

12 According to paragraph 2, in order to survive, a coral reef needs

Ⓐ salt water that is flowing at a moderate speed

Ⓑ water in warm places that is not deep

Ⓒ a large quantity of nutrients in warm water

Ⓓ moderate amounts of sunlight throughout the year

Paragraph 2 is marked with an arrow (⇨).

13 Which of the following can be inferred from paragraph 2 about coral reefs?

Ⓐ There are some that can be found in water that is deeper than fifty meters.

Ⓑ There are a few that are more extensive than the Great Barrier Reef.

Ⓒ They can only survive when the water temperature is at least twenty degrees Celsius.

Ⓓ They are responsible for having created a majority of the Earth's islands in oceans.

Paragraph 2 is marked with an arrow (⇨).

*Glossary

calcium carbonate: a white crystal, often powdery substance found in nature in limestone, chalk, and the secretions of some animals

More Available

14 In paragraph 3, why does the author mention "photosynthesis"?

Ⓐ To state one part of a relationship that occurs in coral reefs

Ⓑ To explain how plants use it to create energy for themselves

Ⓒ To compare the nutrients it produces with those used by zooxanthellae

Ⓓ To prove it is possible for plants several meters underwater to utilize it

Paragraph 3 is marked with an arrow (➡).

15 The word "outlier" in the passage is closest in meaning to

Ⓐ ancestor

Ⓑ original

Ⓒ exception

Ⓓ isolation

➡ The food chain in a reef is similar to that of other ecosystems; plant life supports some species, which are consumed by predators that are in turn hunted by apex predators. Each lifeform in a coral reef ecosystem is dependent upon other lifeforms, creating a vast symbiotic relationship structure. The first and most important relationship involved in the formation of coral reefs is that between coral polyps and plankton called zooxanthellae, a form of single-cell algae. They create food by photosynthesis, which the coral absorbs. In return, the coral provides the zooxanthellae with nutrients they require. The extra food the coral gathers lets it grow quicker than normal, enabling enough fast-growing coral polyps to form a large reef over the course of many years. Despite the enhanced growth, the formation of a reef is a relatively slow process with scientists estimating that the world's extant coral reefs took thousands of years to attain their current forms. The Great Barrier Reef started forming approximately 20,000 years ago, but it is something of an outlier because the majority of reefs are much younger.

*Glossary

apex predator: an animal that is at the top of the food chain and has no natural enemies that hunt it

16 In paragraph 4, the author uses "the crown-of-thorns starfish" as an example of

(A) a predator that preys upon shellfish and small fish residing in coral reefs

(B) an animal that attacks others which devour coral and harm some coral reefs

(C) a creature capable of causing damage to the coral reefs that it lives in

(D) a type of shellfish that filters water in coral reefs and thereby cleanses it

Paragraph 4 is marked with an arrow (➡).

17 According to paragraph 4, fringing coral reefs have seagrasses growing around them because

(A) they provide the nutrient-rich waters which the seagrasses need to develop

(B) they are always located meters from shore, which is where most seagrasses grow

(C) the seagrasses are able to attach themselves to the coral growing in the reefs

(D) the seagrasses are able to attach themselves to the coral growing in the reefs

Paragraph 4 is marked with an arrow (➡).

18 In paragraph 5, the author implies that the Belize Barrier Reef

(A) has had its condition improved thanks to the efforts of humans

(B) is one of the world's largest coral reef systems

(C) could disappear entirely because of the actions of humans

(D) requires immediate action to save it from harmful pollution

Paragraph 5 is marked with an arrow (➪).

➡ Once a reef is established, it attracts other marine lifeforms. Oftentimes, large patches of seagrasses take root alongside the reef. This is typical of fringing coral reefs, which are located near shore. Between the shore and the reef, seagrasses grow in large colonies. The reef provides protection for the seagrasses by preventing them from being uprooted from the seabed by strong waves whereas the seagrasses provide a high level of nutrients which small plankton feed on. These small plankton are afterward consumed by small fish and shellfish. Other marine lifeforms, such as sponges, grow on the reefs themselves. Sponges play a vital role by filtering water, so they break down large nutrient particles into smaller ones the coral and other lifeforms can absorb. Crabs and shrimp reside among the coral, where they gather food from the flowing water. Some of these creatures protect the coral from predators such as the crown-of-thorns starfish, an animal that actually consumes coral and serves as a major threat to some reefs.

➪ As a coral reef expands, its lifeforms diversify. Marine biologists estimate that more than 4,000 fish species live in or around reefs. Small fish are consumed by larger fish, which are subsequently eaten by larger predators, including sharks, sturgeons, and eels. All kinds of seabirds are attracted to the surfaces of reefs due to their abundant food sources. This tremendous amount of life then attracts the world's most dangerous predator: humans. The overfishing of coral reefs has become a major global issue. Humans often destroy delicately balanced coral reef ecosystems by removing certain lifeforms in great numbers. Pollution is another serious threat worldwide because it kills numerous species and promptly upsets the balance in reefs. In recent years, however, efforts to protect coral reefs from fishing and pollution, such as in the endangered Belize Barrier Reef in Central America, have shown promise.

More Available ▲

19 Look at the four squares [■] that indicate where the following sentence could be added to the passage.

On the other hand, others, such as the reefs around Providencia Island in the Caribbean Sea, occupy much less territory.

Where would the sentence best fit?

Click on a square [■] to add the sentence to the passage.

For a coral reef ecosystem to thrive, there must be adequate amounts of sunlight in addition to warm temperatures, so most reefs are located in shallow waters in tropical or subtropical regions. For the most part, they cannot exist in water deeper than fifty meters or in places where the water temperature is below twenty degrees Celsius. **1** Some reefs can reach gargantuan sizes. **2** The world's largest is the Great Barrier Reef, which stretches approximately 2,600 kilometers, off Australia's eastern coast. **3** Some coral reefs grow so much that they ascend above the ocean's surface, creating coral atolls that typically surround large lagoons. **4** One example is the Maldive Islands, which consist of around 1,200 coral atolls in the Indian Ocean.

▼

222

20 **Directions:** An introductory sentence for a brief summary of the passage is provided below. Complete the summary by selecting the THREE answer choices that express the most important ideas of the passage. Some sentences do not belong because they express ideas that are not presented in the passage or are minor ideas in the passage. **This question is worth 2 points.**

> Drag your answer choices to the spaces where they belong. To remove an answer choice, click on it. To review the passage, click on **VIEW TEXT**.

Coral reefs rely upon a number of relationships to form, to attract plant and animal life, and to maintain balance after being established.

-

-

-

ANSWER CHOICES

1. The vast number of species living in coral reefs attracts humans, who are causing severe damage to coral reefs located all around the world.

2. The plants that grow in and around coral reefs provide sustenance for some fish, which are then consumed by larger ones.

3. The largest of the Earth's coral reefs, such as the Great Barrier Reef, may take several thousand years to develop.

4. Sharks, sturgeons, and eels are some of the top predators that hunt the smaller creatures which can be found living in coral reefs.

5. Coral polyps and zooxanthellae provide assistance to one another since they have a symbiotic relationship, and this allows coral reefs to grow.

6. While a large number of flora and fauna can be found living in coral reefs, there are typically only a few species of each to be found in them.

Reforestation Efforts

Mount St. Helens in 2015

Forests disappear for numerous reasons, including natural causes such as wildfires, volcanic eruptions, and insect invasions as well as manmade ones such as <u>clear-cutting</u> for lumber and chopping down trees to make room for agriculture and other developments. While some forests vanish forever, others are rejuvenated through natural processes or with human assistance. The manner in which they recover varies from place to place; however, although the regions are once again covered by trees, the results are not always ideal, and the forests do not normally resemble their past selves.

Natural disasters can result in tremendous amounts of damage to forests, and those destroyed in this manner can typically be reforested only through natural means. One example of a forest that suffered from a catastrophe caused by <u>Mother Nature</u> is the area around the volcano Mount St. Helens in Washington, USA. It violently erupted in May 1980 and devastated a large region surrounding it. Approximately fifty square kilometers of forest were destroyed. Since that time, the land around the volcano has slowly but steadily recovered. Initially, the soil was damaged and had extremely low levels of nitrogen, a nutrient necessary for plant growth. Some of the first plants to reappear were those that extract nitrogen from the air rather than the soil. One was the prairie lupine, a small purple flower. Plants like it attracted insects and small herbivores, which, in turn, deposited organic matter into the soil. This activity gradually increased the soil's nitrogen level, permitting other plants to have sustained growth. Eventually, trees began growing on the fringes of the devastated area and continually expanded their areas of growth. While not yet fully recovered, one day, the region around Mount St. Helens may return to its former beauty.

Some places, on the other hand, have been so deforested by logging and human encroachment that they require human assistance to recover. In South America, the Atlantic Forest once covered an area estimated at more than one million square kilometers as it extended down the Atlantic coast of Brazil,

Paraguay, and Argentina. Over the course of several centuries, the inhabitants chopped down parts of the forest with little thought regarding management. Now, it covers an area of fewer than one hundred thousand square kilometers, a reduction of more than ninety percent of its original size. Conservation efforts by governments and other groups have begun rebuilding the forest though. Some groups collect seedlings from surviving areas and raise the plants in nurseries. When they become large enough, teams take the small trees to the periphery of the forest and plant them, thus expanding the size of the forest. Although it will require decades for the Atlantic Forest to recover, the volunteers have made an outstanding start by planting hundreds of thousands of trees. The trees are of numerous species, which will ensure a robust forest ecosystem.

A variety of species is important because planting a single species or only a few will not ensure the ideal recovery of an ecosystem. For instance, during World War II in the 1940s, Japan had trouble obtaining fuel for its war effort, so the Japanese cut down large swaths of forested areas to burn the trees for fuel. When the war ended, the Japanese immediately set to work rebuilding their vanished forests. Since they needed lumber to rebuild damaged cities, they mostly planted two types of trees: cypress trees and cedar trees. Soon afterward, Japanese business leaders started acquiring cheaper sources of lumber from Southeast Asia, so it was no longer necessary to cut down the trees they had planted. Today, more than forty percent of Japan's forests are comprised of those two types of trees, resulting in an astounding lack of biodiversity in Japan's forests that has created various problems. For example, many streams in cedar and cypress forests lack fish. The reason is that cypress and cedar trees attract few insects and do not drop much plant matter into the water, so fish are deprived of critical food sources. Another problem is that each spring, the trees release large quantities of pollen into the atmosphere, resulting in mass outbreaks of hay fever. Many people call in sick to work, making the country's economy suffer.

*Glossary

clear-cut: to chop down every tree in a certain area
Mother Nature: the personification of natural forces as a nurturing individual

21 The word "rejuvenated" in the passage is closest in meaning to

(A) replaced

(B) restored

(C) resented

(D) reported

22 In paragraph 1, the author's description of forests mentions all of the following EXCEPT:

(A) how they look in comparison to their previous selves when they grow back

(B) some of the reasons that humans have been known to cause them to disappear

(C) the amount of time that it takes for them to grow back after having been destroyed

(D) a few of the natural disasters that are capable of destroying them

Paragraph 1 is marked with an arrow (➡).

Reforestation Efforts

➡ Forests disappear for numerous reasons, including natural causes such as wildfires, volcanic eruptions, and insect invasions as well as manmade ones such as clear-cutting for lumber and chopping down trees to make room for agriculture and other developments. While some forests vanish forever, others are rejuvenated through natural processes or with human assistance. The manner in which they recover varies from place to place; however, although the regions are once again covered by trees, the results are not always ideal, and the forests do not normally resemble their past selves.

*Glossary

clear-cut: to chop down every tree in a certain area

REVIEW

HELP

BACK

NEXT

HIDE TIME 00:54:00

More Available

23 In paragraph 2, the author mentions "the prairie lupine" as an example of

Ⓐ the plant that is the most responsible for attracting animals to a devastated area

Ⓑ one of the first species of plants to grow around Mount St. Helens after it erupted

Ⓒ a species of tree that managed to survive a violent volcanic eruption

Ⓓ a plant that is able to replenish the soil better than other plants can

Paragraph 2 is marked with an arrow (➡).

24 Which of the following can be inferred from paragraph 2 about volcanic eruptions?

Ⓐ They can cause the removal of nitrogen from the soil in the land that they affect.

Ⓑ They are the natural disasters most responsible for deforesting places around the world.

Ⓒ They kill large numbers of humans and animals when they erupt without warning.

Ⓓ They destroy the land so much that human assistance is required to restore it.

Paragraph 2 is marked with an arrow (➡).

➡ Natural disasters can result in tremendous amounts of damage to forests, and those destroyed in this manner can typically be reforested only through natural means. One example of a forest that suffered from a catastrophe caused by Mother Nature is the area around the volcano Mount St. Helens in Washington, USA. It violently erupted in May 1980 and devastated a large region surrounding it. Approximately fifty square kilometers of forest were destroyed. Since that time, the land around the volcano has slowly but steadily recovered. Initially, the soil was damaged and had extremely low levels of nitrogen, a nutrient necessary for plant growth. Some of the first plants to reappear were those that extract nitrogen from the air rather than the soil. One was the prairie lupine, a small purple flower. Plants like it attracted insects and small herbivores, which, in turn, deposited organic matter into the soil. This activity gradually increased the soil's nitrogen level, permitting other plants to have sustained growth. Eventually, trees began growing on the fringes of the devastated area and continually expanded their areas of growth. While not yet fully recovered, one day, the region around Mount St. Helens may return to its former beauty.

*Glossary

Mother Nature: the personification of natural forces as a nurturing individual

25 The word "periphery" in the passage is closest in meaning to

(A) center

(B) far side

(C) edge

(D) shore

26 According to paragraph 3, which of the following is true about the Atlantic Forest?

(A) Logging and farming have become banned activities within the forest.

(B) The deforestation of the land required only a few decades to occur.

(C) The actions of humans have reduced it in size by a considerable amount.

(D) Local governments are paying groups to plant seedlings in the forest.

Paragraph 3 is marked with an arrow (➡).

➡ Some places, on the other hand, have been so deforested by logging and human encroachment that they require human assistance to recover. In South America, the Atlantic Forest once covered an area estimated at more than one million square kilometers as it extended down the Atlantic coast of Brazil, Paraguay, and Argentina. Over the course of several centuries, the inhabitants chopped down parts of the forest with little thought regarding management. Now, it covers an area of fewer than one hundred thousand square kilometers, a reduction of more than ninety percent of its original size. Conservation efforts by governments and other groups have begun rebuilding the forest though. Some groups collect seedlings from surviving areas and raise the plants in nurseries. When they become large enough, teams take the small trees to the periphery of the forest and plant them, thus expanding the size of the forest. Although it will require decades for the Atlantic Forest to recover, the volunteers have made an outstanding start by planting hundreds of thousands of trees. The trees are of numerous species, which will ensure a robust forest ecosystem.

27 According to paragraph 4, Japanese forests disappeared during World War II because

- Ⓐ many trees were infected with a variety of diseases that killed most of them
- Ⓑ they were destroyed in various battles and bombing campaigns in the country
- Ⓒ many trees were cut down in order to be utilized in the Japanese war effort
- Ⓓ they burned down in enormous fires that were started by the enemies of Japan

Paragraph 4 is marked with an arrow (➡).

28 According to paragraph 4, one problem with many forests in present-day Japan is that

- Ⓐ few people are interested in restoring them and making them more diverse
- Ⓑ they are devoid of lots of animals since the trees in them provide little or no food
- Ⓒ most of the trees are unable to resist various diseases, so they often die in large numbers
- Ⓓ the trees in them are cut down for their lumber, so the forests are shrinking in size

Paragraph 4 is marked with an arrow (➡).

➡ A variety of species is important because planting a single species or only a few will not ensure the ideal recovery of an ecosystem. For instance, during World War II in the 1940s, Japan had trouble obtaining fuel for its war effort, so the Japanese cut down large swaths of forested areas to burn the trees for fuel. When the war ended, the Japanese immediately set to work rebuilding their vanished forests. Since they needed lumber to rebuild damaged cities, they mostly planted two types of trees: cypress trees and cedar trees. Soon afterward, Japanese business leaders started acquiring cheaper sources of lumber from Southeast Asia, so it was no longer necessary to cut down the trees they had planted. Today, more than forty percent of Japan's forests are comprised of those two types of trees, resulting in an astounding lack of biodiversity in Japan's forests that has created various problems. For example, many streams in cedar and cypress forests lack fish. The reason is that cypress and cedar trees attract few insects and do not drop much plant matter into the water, so fish are deprived of critical food sources. Another problem is that each spring, the trees release large quantities of pollen into the atmosphere, resulting in mass outbreaks of hay fever. Many people call in sick to work, making the country's economy suffer.

PASSAGE 3

Q
REVIEW

? HELP

< BACK

> NEXT

HIDE TIME 00:54:00

End ▲

29 Look at the four squares [■] that indicate where the following sentence could be added to the passage.

These replanted forests were then left alone and permitted to continue growing.

Where would the sentence best fit?

Click on a square [■] to add the sentence to the passage.

A variety of species is important because planting a single species or only a few will not ensure the ideal recovery of an ecosystem. For instance, during World War II in the 1940s, Japan had trouble obtaining fuel for its war effort, so the Japanese cut down large swaths of forested areas to burn the trees for fuel. When the war ended, the Japanese immediately set to work rebuilding their vanished forests. Since they needed lumber to rebuild damaged cities, they mostly planted two types of trees: cypress trees and cedar trees. Soon afterward, Japanese business leaders started acquiring cheaper sources of lumber from Southeast Asia, so it was no longer necessary to cut down the trees they had planted. **1** Today, more than forty percent of Japan's forests are comprised of those two types of trees, resulting in an astounding lack of biodiversity in Japan's forests that has created various problems. **2** For example, many streams in cedar and cypress forests lack fish. **3** The reason is that cypress and cedar trees attract few insects and do not drop much plant matter into the water, so fish are deprived of critical food sources. **4** Another problem is that each spring, the trees release large quantities of pollen into the atmosphere, resulting in mass outbreaks of hay fever. Many people call in sick to work, making the country's economy suffer.

VIEW TEXT

REVIEW

HELP

BACK

NEXT

HIDE TIME 00:54:00

30 **Directions:** Select the appropriate statements from the answer choices and match them to the forest to which they relate. TWO of the answer choices will NOT be used. **This question is worth 4 points.**

Drag your answer choices to the spaces where they belong. To remove an answer choice, click on it. To review the passage, click on **VIEW TEXT**.

ANSWER CHOICES

1. Replanted with only a couple of types of trees for the most part

2. Suffered serious damage due to numerous wildfires

3. Reduced to a tiny amount of land compared to what it once occupied

4. Can be found in parts of the territory of several different countries

5. Recovered in part due to plants putting nutrients back into the soil

6. Suffered tremendously due to a volcanic eruption

7. Lost large numbers of trees because of diseases imported by invasive species

8. Incurred harm because of an ongoing military conflict

9. Currently being restored by both governments and other groups

FOREST

Mount St. Helens (Select 2)

-
-

Atlantic Forest (Select 3)

-
-
-

Japanese Forests (Select 2)

-
-

AUTHORS

Michael A. Putlack
- MA in History, Tufts University, Medford, MA, USA
- Expert test developer of TOEFL, TOEIC, and TEPS
- Main author of the Darakwon *How to Master Skills for the TOEFL® iBT* series and *TOEFL® MAP* series

Stephen Poirier
- Candidate for PhD in History, University of Western Ontario, Canada
- Certificate of Professional Technical Writing, Carleton University, Canada
- Co-author of the Darakwon *How to Master Skills for the TOEFL® iBT* series and *TOEFL® MAP* series

Allen C. Jacobs
- BS in Physics, Presbyterian College, Clinton, SC, USA
- BCE in Civil Engineering, Auburn University, Auburn, AL, USA
- MS in Civil Engineering, University of Alabama, Tuscaloosa, AL, USA

Decoding the TOEFL® iBT
Actual Test READING 2 NEW TOEFL® EDITION

Publisher Chung Kyudo
Editor Kim Minju
Authors Michael A. Putlack, Stephen Poirier, Allen C. Jacobs
Proofreader Michael A. Putlack
Designers Koo Soojung, Park Sunyoung

First published in March 2020
By Darakwon, Inc.
Darakwon Bldg., 211, Munbal-ro, Paju-si, Gyeonggi-do 10881
Republic of Korea
Tel: 82-2-736-2031 (Ext. 250)
Fax: 82-2-732-2037

ISBN 978-89-277-0867-4 14740
978-89-277-0862-9 14740 (set)

www.darakwon.co.kr

Photo Credits
Kmusser (p. 69)
https://commons.wikimedia.org/wiki/File:Tigr-euph.png
Drone Explorer (p. 109), Artur Bogacki (p. 157) / Shutterstock.com

Components Test Book / Answer Book
9 8 7 6 5 4 3   23 24 25 26 27